Cambridge Elements

Elements in Forensic Linguistics
edited by
Tim Grant
Aston University
Tammy Gales
Hofstra University

TRUST, DISCOURSE, AND CORPORATE CORRUPTION

The Case of Enron

Matteo Fuoli
University of Birmingham

Adam Nix
University of Birmingham

Alicia Wickert
University of Birmingham

Annina Van Riper
University of Birmingham

Shaftesbury Road, Cambridge CB2 8EA, United Kingdom

One Liberty Plaza, 20th Floor, New York, NY 10006, USA

477 Williamstown Road, Port Melbourne, VIC 3207, Australia

314–321, 3rd Floor, Plot 3, Splendor Forum, Jasola District Centre, New Delhi – 110025, India

103 Penang Road, #05–06/07, Visioncrest Commercial, Singapore 238467

Cambridge University Press is part of Cambridge University Press & Assessment, a department of the University of Cambridge.

We share the University's mission to contribute to society through the pursuit of education, learning and research at the highest international levels of excellence.

www.cambridge.org
Information on this title: www.cambridge.org/9781009665971
DOI: 10.1017/9781009665957

© Matteo Fuoli, Adam Nix, Alicia Wickert, and Annina Van Riper 2025

This publication is in copyright. Subject to statutory exception and to the provisions of relevant collective licensing agreements, with the exception of the Creative Commons version the link for which is provided below, no reproduction of any part may take place without the written permission of Cambridge University Press & Assessment.

An online version of this work is published at doi.org/10.1017/9781009665957 under a Creative Commons Open Access license CC-BY-NC 4.0 which permits re-use, distribution and reproduction in any medium for non-commercial purposes providing appropriate credit to the original work is given and any changes made are indicated. To view a copy of this license visit https://creativecommons.org/licenses/by-nc/4.0

When citing this work, please include a reference to the DOI 10.1017/9781009665957

First published 2025

A catalogue record for this publication is available from the British Library

ISBN 978-1-009-66597-1 Hardback
ISBN 978-1-009-66594-0 Paperback
ISSN 2634-7334 (online)
ISSN 2634-7326 (print)

Cambridge University Press & Assessment has no responsibility for the persistence or accuracy of URLs for external or third-party internet websites referred to in this publication and does not guarantee that any content on such websites is, or will remain, accurate or appropriate.

For EU product safety concerns, contact us at Calle de José Abascal, 56, 1°, 28003 Madrid, Spain, or email eugpsr@cambridge.org

Trust, Discourse, and Corporate Corruption

The Case of Enron

Elements in Forensic Linguistics

DOI: 10.1017/9781009665957
First published online: December 2025

Matteo Fuoli
University of Birmingham

Adam Nix
University of Birmingham

Alicia Wickert
University of Birmingham

Annina Van Riper
University of Birmingham

Author for correspondence: Matteo Fuoli, m.fuoli@bham.ac.uk

Abstract: In this Element, the authors propose a new framework for studying how trust is built and manipulated in discourse and apply it to one of the most notorious cases of corporate misconduct in history: the Enron fraud. The framework outlines the discursive strategies speakers commonly use to manage trust, providing a tool for examining how language shapes relationships and enables wrongdoing in both physical and digital environments. The analysis, which focuses on a previously unexplored corpus of telephone conversations involving Enron traders, uncovers the discursive mechanisms through which Enron managed trust both internally and externally while manipulating California's energy markets. The findings not only provide novel insights into the Enron case but also advance our understanding of the linguistic and pragmatic foundations of trust and the relationship between discourse, trust, and corporate corruption. This title is also available as Open Access on Cambridge Core.

This Element also has a video abstract: www.cambridge.org/EIFL_Fuoli_abstract

Keywords: discursive trust management, manipulation, deception, corporate fraud, Enron

© Matteo Fuoli, Adam Nix, Alicia Wickert, and Annina Van Riper 2025

ISBNs: 9781009665971 (HB), 9781009665940 (PB), 9781009665957 (OC)
ISSNs: 2634-7334 (online), 2634-7326 (print)

Contents

Series Preface   1

1 Introduction   2

2 Theoretical Background   11

3 The Enron Case Study   17

4 Methodology   28

5 Trust Management in the Enron Trader Tapes Corpus   35

6 Discussion   70

7 Conclusion   78

References   81

Series Preface

The Elements in Forensic Linguistics series from Cambridge University Press publishes across five main topic areas (1) investigative and forensic text analysis; (2) the study of spoken linguistic practices in legal contexts; (3) the linguistic analysis of written legal texts; (4) interdisciplinary research in related fields; (5) historical development and reflection often through explorations of the origins, development, and scope of the field in various countries and regions. *Trust, discourse, and corporate corruption: The case of Enron* by Matteo Fuoli, Adam Nix, Alicia Wickert, and Annina Van Riper is perhaps hard to categorise against these topic areas. It is relevant to investigative text analysis, but focused on spoken business telephone conversations. These ought to have been legally constrained, but some of them were supportive of the enormous corruption behind the Enron collapse. The Element thus, is also deeply interdisciplinary, explaining the corporate context in which these conversations took place.

As the authors point out in their introduction, "*Enron traders could not have manipulated California's electricity markets on their own. Their strategies relied on securing the trust of external organizations*". They thus provide a linguistic description of trust-building practices that lead these external others on a path to act in ways that might have been against their better judgment, and ultimately in support of widespread corruption. In this sense, this Element links directly to Lis Carter's Element, *The Language of Romance Crimes*, in which she sets out the grooming process and the securing of trust, through which a victim is convinced to act against their own best interests. Partly because they can access so much data, Fuoli and colleagues are able to go beyond the linguistic descriptions of individual conversations and their interactional structures, to build a model of the pragmatics of trust, involving an understanding of the rhetorical moves that support five core processes or "macro functions" drawn from their analysis of the behavioral sciences. This is a significant contribution to the field that can be tested beyond the context of the Enron corporate failure into other areas of forensic linguistics where trust building and persuasion are key, whether this be in romance fraud, child grooming, or radicalisation. As such, this Element will be a relevant and significant contribution beyond forensic linguistics, across many disciplines including behavioral science, forensic psychology, cybersecurity, and business studies with direct interest in fraud and how it occurs.

Tim Grant
Series Editor

1 Introduction

1.1 A linguistic Approach to Trust

Trust is essential for a thriving society, yet paradoxically, it also plays a critical role in enabling various forms of crime, from corporate fraud (Rhodes 2016) and bribery (Graeff 2004) to illegal cartels (Bertrand & Lumineau 2016), romance scams (Carter 2024), and online child sexual grooming (Lorenzo-Dus et al. 2023). To achieve their goals while evading detection, offenders must cultivate trust with a range of people, including victims, accomplices (unwitting or otherwise), and, in some cases, even regulatory and law enforcement authorities. Verbal communication is central to this trust-building process; through discourse, people form bonds, make commitments, demonstrate competence, and share confidential information. Thus, uncovering the linguistic mechanisms of trust is crucial for understanding and effectively combating crime in both the physical world and cyberspace.

Although trust is central to many forms of criminal activity and is largely established through discourse, the linguistic mechanisms underpinning it remain poorly understood. Existing research is patchy and lacks a comprehensive and coherent framework for the analysis of how trust is managed in and through verbal interaction. This Element addresses this gap by proposing a new approach to the study of discursive trust management. We develop our framework inductively via a detailed linguistic analysis of one of the most notorious and well-documented historical cases of corporate corruption: the Enron fraud.

Enron, once one of the largest energy companies in the world, rose to prominence during the 1990s through aggressive trading and a reputation for innovation in the energy sector. However, the company's fortunes turned in the early 2000s when its widespread fraudulent practices began to unravel. The company had been hiding massive debts and inflating profits through complex accounting schemes, misleading investors and regulators. But the company's misconduct went beyond "creative" accounting. On June 25, 2003, nearly two years after Enron's bankruptcy, the United States Federal Energy Regulatory Commission (FERC) delivered a further blow to its shattered legacy, finding that Enron's West Power division had manipulated California's wholesale electricity markets through various "gaming" practices (FERC 2003a). Enron exploited flaws in California's newly deregulated energy markets, boosting its profits while fueling one of the most severe energy crises in US history, during which the State faced acute energy supply shortages, widespread rolling blackouts, and skyrocketing electricity prices.

Enron traders could not have manipulated California's electricity markets on their own. Their strategies relied on securing the trust of external organizations to gain access to and control the State's energy infrastructure. Specifically, Enron pioneered financial service provision within the US energy industry, managing California's new markets on behalf of firms that largely lacked competitive market experience and financial capabilities. It was in this capacity that Enron formed partnerships with companies, often through "consultancy" relationships with profit-sharing agreements, and entered into various long and short-term transactional relationships throughout California and the western States (FERC 2007). These relationships allowed the company to directly control electricity flows and manipulate market conditions. For example, Enron traders regularly instructed partners to turn specific electricity generation units off, artificially constraining supply and driving up market prices (Nix et al. 2022). These coordinated market moves were often discussed and arranged on the phone, as shown in the following authentic snippet from a call between Enron's BW and Rich, an employee from an electric utility company.[1]

Extract 1

```
1   BW:   All right, man. I'm n - this is gonna be a word of mouth kind
2         of thing.
3   R:    OK.
4   BW:   Um, tonight, ah, when you finish your normal QF, so for hour
5         ending one -
6   R:    Right.
7   BW:   - it'll actually be tomorrow -
8   R:    Right.
9   BW:   -ah, we want you guys to get a little creative-
10  R:    OK.
11  BW:   - and come up with a reason to go down.
12  R:    OK.
13  BW:   Anything you want to do over there? Any-
14  R:    Ah -
15  BW:   - cleaning, anything like that?
16  R:    Yeah. Yeah. There's some stuff that we could be doin' tonight.
17  BW:   That's good.
```

Extract 1 is taken from a collection of typed transcripts of 505 internal and external phone conversations involving Enron employees during the California energy crisis, which were released by FERC as part of the legal proceedings against Enron West Power. This is the corpus we will examine in our case study and use as a testbed to develop our framework for the analysis of discursive trust

---

[1] In this and all extracts presented in the Element, double initials denote traders from Enron West Power, while single initials represent external speakers, including employees from Enron Corporation's main headquarters in Houston. In the body text, we identify Enron traders by their initials and refer to external speakers by their full names. To protect the privacy of the individuals involved, we have redacted all surnames and company names from the excerpts.

management. Approximately 415,000 words in size, the 'Enron Trader Tapes Corpus' (ETTC) is the largest known spoken language corpus derived from a context of known illegal activity. Access to such clandestine conversations is rare, and available datasets tend to be limited in scope. This makes the ETTC an invaluable resource not only for our specific case study but also for research into how spoken interaction functions within criminal contexts more generally. The corpus, so far unexplored from a linguistic perspective, affords a unique opportunity to examine how trust develops in real time through verbal interaction and how it facilitates the formation and management of multi-organizational corruption networks.

To achieve this goal, however, we first need to establish an analytical framework that captures the broad range of discursive strategies speakers use in interaction, not only to build trust but also to probe, repair, and maintain it – in other words, to *manage* trust. Such a framework will not only enable us to flesh out the pragmatics of discursive trust work, but also to infer the level of trust in a relationship based on the participants' linguistic behavior. Extract 1, for example, suggests a high level of trust between the Enron trader and his interlocutor. This trust is evident in several features of their language. For instance, BW introduces his request by emphasizing its confidential nature (lines 1–2). Such framing implies that he trusts Rich to keep the matter private, as any disclosure could lead to serious legal consequences. BW's use of the informal "you guys" (line 9) further indicates a sense of camaraderie and familiarity between them, which in turn potentially helps reinforce their bond. Rich's unhesitating acceptance of BW's proposal (lines 10, 12, 16) also serves as a tacit display of trust, which BW acknowledges with the approving remark, "that's good" (line 17).

Not all interactions between Enron traders and external actors went as smoothly as in Extract 1, however. In Extract 2, for example, an operator at the California Independent System Operator (ISO), the entity responsible for managing the State's electricity grid and wholesale power market, accuses Enron of scheduling a speculative energy transmission in and out of California without confirmed customers. He repeatedly challenges the accuracy of Enron's explanation, expressing distrust through questions (lines 1–2), directives (lines 11–12, 14), and even a threat to block the schedule (lines 11, 16–17). In response, the Enron trader defensively denies any intention to export energy out of State (line 3) and offers an alternative account of the transaction to reassure the operator of its legitimacy. He explains that he bought 44 megawatts of electricity from a market (the "PX") located in Palo Verde to supply his customers in California (lines 3–4, 7–8), not to export it, and claims that the ISO itself is the designated recipient (line 13, the "sink"). This example starkly contrasts with the previous one; it shows that to achieve its illicit aims, Enron not only needed to cultivate trust with partners and clients but also had to ensure that regulatory authorities and other market entities trusted the company enough to perceive its actions as routine and unproblematic. The example also clearly shows that trust is dynamic and often requires repair during interactions.

Extract 2

```
1    M:    What customers? You don't have any. How can you have customers
2          if you're already exporting 44 megawatts?
3    MU:   I'm not exporting. I bought those megawatts outside at Palo
4          Verde from the PX. The PX sold me megawatts at Palo Verde.
6    M:    OK and that – and that you're gonna – OK.
7    MU:   And I'm taking those megawatts that I purchased at Palo Verde
8          to serve my customers in California.
9    M:    OK, tell you what, Mike. If you have a source, if have a sink
10         for me at Palo Verde for the 44 megawatts that's exporting,
11         then I won't cut that to zero and you have five minutes to find
12         that for me –
13   MU:   The sink is the ISO.
14   M:    If you have an – if you have a s – just listen to me 'cause you
15         have – you have five minutes. And then if you have a source for
16         the import coming in at Palo Verde, then I won't cut that
17         schedule.
```

These examples, though small, clearly demonstrate the crucial role of language in negotiating and managing trust. They also provide an initial glimpse into the potential of linguistic analysis as a valuable tool for uncovering the inner workings of trust. When applied to a forensic context, such as a historical corporate corruption case like Enron, this type of linguistic analysis can yield new insights into the linguistic and interpersonal dynamics at play, potentially enhancing our understanding of and approach to various forms of crime. However, as we discuss in the next section, forensic linguistic research on trust remains in its early stages, as does our overall understanding of the linguistic mechanisms and features involved in discursive trust management.

1.2 Previous Research on Trust in Forensic Linguistics

To date, research in forensic linguistics has not focused directly on trust, nor has it attempted to develop a comprehensive framework for analyzing discursive trust management. Instead, trust has mainly been studied as one aspect of the related, yet distinct, phenomenon of manipulation. For example, Lorenzo-Dus and colleagues have examined the discursive tactics used by online sexual groomers to lure their victims (Lorenzo-Dus 2022; Lorenzo-Dus et al. 2016, 2020, 2023; Lorenzo-Dus & Izura 2017; Lorenzo-Dus & Kinzel 2019). One of the four core tactics deployed by groomers is what the authors call "deceptive trust development", where trust is intentionally built to enable sexual abuse rather than to establish a genuine relationship (Lorenzo-Dus et al. 2023). Deceptive trust development is accomplished through a set of specific sub-tactics. These include engaging in discussions about shared interests and activities, offering compliments, and making small talk (Lorenzo-Dus et al. 2023). An important insight from this work, which we carry over into our own research, is the significance of emotions and bonding as central components of trust building. This underscores the fact that, as discussed in more detail in Section 2.1, trust is not merely a cognitive phenomenon but also, and to a large extent, an affective one (McAllister 1995). Another useful insight is the importance of vulnerability in the trust-building process. In sexual grooming discourse, vulnerability is weaponized for manipulative purposes. Groomers frequently communicate personal emotions and insecurities, revealing their own apparent vulnerabilities as a calculated strategy to win the trust of their targets (Lorenzo-Dus et al. 2023).

While Lorenzo-Dus and colleagues' work provides useful observations, it offers only a partial picture of the discursive processes and features involved in trust management. First of all, the authors focus exclusively on trust building for manipulative purposes. Trust management, however, is a more complex discursive activity that involves not only building trust but also probing, maintaining, and repairing it. Moreover, while discourse can certainly be used to manipulate other people's trust for personal gain, not all discursive trust management has a deceptive purpose, even in the context of wrongdoing. For example, it is implausible that in all interactions where trust was at stake, Enron traders sought to deceptively manipulate other Enron traders or external partners. In fact, given that trust is a fundamental element of workplace interactions and a critical enabler of collaboration (Costa et al. 2018), we expect to observe numerous instances of genuine trust-building that are not directly aimed at manipulating others for illicit purposes, but rather at fostering positive and mutually beneficial relationships. Lastly, since Lorenzo-Dus and colleagues did not set out to develop a general framework of trust but rather to explore how trust is established within a specific context of cybercrime, their account is understandably limited in scope. In contrast, our aim is to build a more comprehensive and broadly applicable typology of discursive trust management strategies.

Although not the primary focus, trust is also a central theme in Carter's (2024) analysis of manipulation tactics in the context of romance fraud. Carter (2024) demonstrates that trust is a crucial tool and prerequisite for fraudsters to manipulate their victims and ultimately exploit them financially. As with studies on online sexual grooming, Carter (2024) identifies a range of deceptive trust-building strategies used by fraudsters, such as feigning vulnerability, performing honesty through self-disclosure narratives, and appealing to religious values. Carter's (2024) work emphasizes the central role of language in trust-building and as a means for individuals to assess other people's trustworthiness. This is especially relevant in cyberspace, where language is often the only tool available for evaluating whether someone can be trusted. However, because trust is not the central focus, this study does not provide a systematic overview of the linguistic features related to trust. Moreover, trust is not explicitly defined and is often conflated with the related, but distinct, concept of 'rapport'.

Another area of cybercrime examined in forensic linguistics in relation to trust is drug trafficking on the dark web. Lorenzo-Dus and Di Cristofaro (2018) investigate how trust is constructed in crypto-drug markets using corpus-assisted discourse analysis and data from the "Silk Road" community forums. They find that community members project expertise by showcasing their personal experience (e.g., providing detailed accounts of drug-related experiences) and by referring to external sources of knowledge (e.g., referencing scientific or media publications). Moreover, they communicate integrity and benevolence by giving and seeking advice on drug use, geared towards minimizing health risks. This research highlights the importance of language as a tool for constructing and performing a trustworthy identity, offering valuable insights into trust dynamics within the specific context of crypto-drug markets. However, the analysis is context-specific and does not provide recommendations for broadly applicable categories of linguistic features that could be used in our own work.

Beyond these studies, other research in forensic linguistics mentions trust only in passing. For instance, Chiang and Grant (2017: 111) find that one of the ways in which sexual groomers build rapport with their victims is by "using and eliciting statements of trust and reassurance". Childs and Walsh (2017) discuss the use of self-disclosure by police officers in interviews with children reporting alleged sexual offenses as a means of eliciting trust from interviewees. Wilson and Walsh (2019) also touch upon trust as a potential source of conflict in interpreter-assisted police interviews. Their study, however, is based on questionnaire data and does not include a linguistic analysis of authentic police interviews.

Other concepts related to, but distinct from, trust have received more attention in the forensic linguistic literature. One such concept is rapport, which has been analyzed as a key feature of police interviews (Childs & Walsh 2017; Fogarty et al. 2013; Pablos-Ortega 2021; Pounds 2019) and in online child grooming discourse (Chiang et al. 2020; Chiang & Grant 2017). However, a key issue with this body of research is the lack of explicit definitions for rapport and scant detail about the linguistic features associated with it. The definitions that do exist are often inconsistent. For example, Childs and Walsh (2017) define rapport as a "harmonious, empathetic, or sympathetic relation or connection to another self", while Chiang and Grant (2017: 111) describe rapport building as "attempts to establish and maintain a friendship/relationship with a target". While trust and rapport are undoubtedly related, they are not synonymous. As discussed in Section 2.1, trust involves elements of vulnerability and risk, which may not necessarily be part of rapport. Moreover, rapport does not seem to fully capture what is happening in Extract 2, where what is at stake is the trustworthiness of the Enron trader and the credibility of his account, rather than "harmony" or "friendship". However, in Extract 1, there is evidence of both good rapport and mutual trust between the speakers, indicating some overlap between these constructs.

Another concept related to trust that has received considerable attention in forensic linguistics is 'persuasion', particularly in the context of extremist discourses (Baker et al. 2021; Benítez-Castro & Hidalgo-Tenorio 2022; Etaywe & Zappavigna 2022, 2024; Ladd & Goodwin 2022; Lorenzo-Dus & Macdonald 2018; Lorenzo-Dus & Nouri 2021; Macdonald & Lorenzo-Dus 2021; Prentice et al. 2012). This body of research has made significant progress in revealing how extremists use rhetorical and discursive strategies such as formal language (Baker et al. 2021), evaluative language (Etaywe & Zappavigna 2022), and persuasive arguments (Ladd & Goodwin 2022) to radicalize individuals and promote terrorism. But while trust is undoubtedly a crucial enabler of radicalization, as extremists must earn their targets' trust to steer their behavior, it is important to distinguish it from the concept of persuasion. Persuasion, like manipulation, is a communicative function. Trust, on the other hand, is a psychological and relational construct. Persuasion can serve as a means to win someone's trust, but it is not the same as trust itself. Moreover, discursive trust management extends beyond merely persuading others to trust. As will be discussed later, expressions of skepticism and distrust, like those observed in Extract 2, are also integral to this process. These verbal acts, however, are not necessarily persuasive in nature.

Finally, Newsome-Chandler and Grant (2024) apply the concepts of 'power' and 'authority' to understand relational dynamics within anonymous online criminal networks and the roles of individuals in these communities. There is some overlap between trust and power, but while trust is often important for gaining power and influence, it is not always necessary. In authoritarian contexts, for instance, power is exercised through fear, coercion, or intimidation rather than trust. Authority can be viewed as an aspect of an individual's trustworthiness, potentially serving as a precursor to trust. But while displaying authority in language can foster trust, it is just one of many ways to do so. Moreover, Newsome-Chandler and Grant's (2023) definition of authority, which essentially equates to expertise, captures only one of the three fundamental aspects of trustworthiness, as discussed in Section 2.1. Lastly, as already mentioned, discursive trust management encompasses more than just trust building; it also involves maintaining, reinforcing, and repairing trust dynamically as interactions unfold.

1.3 Previous Research on Trust in Discourse Studies

The topic of trust remains relatively new in discourse studies but has drawn increasing attention in recent years. Research in this area can be broadly divided into three main strands. The first strand includes conversation analysis work exploring how trust is negotiated in various interactional contexts, such as asylum interviews (Linell & Keselman 2011), doctor-patient interactions (Antaki & Finlay 2013; O'Grady & Candlin 2013), child protection meetings (Hall et al. 2013), and job interviews (Kuśmierczyk 2014). These studies highlight the importance of trust as a feature of communication across different professional and social settings. They show that trust is contextual and inherently dialogic; speakers dynamically co-construct trust by engaging with and responding to each other's turns as the conversation unfolds. They also point to various linguistic features involved in discursive trust management, such as pragmatic moves like explaining and empathizing, the choice of address terms, and the use of humor and verbal backchannels. However, this literature tends to focus on individual or a limited set of features within specific interactional contexts and has not produced a comprehensive, widely applicable framework for the analysis of discursive trust management.

Studies within the second research strand use text and corpus analysis to examine the linguistics of trust in monologic communication, focusing primarily on the strategies employed in institutional discourses to communicate trustworthiness. For instance, Fuoli (2018b) investigates how companies use 'stance' expressions in their annual reports to convey integrity and competence, fostering trust with investors and other stakeholders. Bondi and Nocella (2023) analyze how UK and Italian rail companies used language to encourage people to trust public transport during the COVID-19 pandemic. Wang and Yao (2022) focus on the pandemic, too, examining how Chinese authorities used language strategically in their social media communications to build public trust. This body of work offers valuable insights that can inform the development of our analytical framework. It demonstrates how language can be used strategically to communicate trustworthiness and pinpoints specific linguistic features that can serve this purpose, in particular, evaluative and affective language. However, due to its focus on written and monologic institutional discourse, the applicability of this research to dialogic interaction is inherently limited.

The third research strand uses sociologically inspired discourse analysis and linguistic-ethnographic methods to explore how trust is understood, discussed, and achieved in various settings. Researchers in this field analyze a wide range of discursive data, including qualitative interviews (Anderson & Petersen 2013), personal narratives (Crichton 2013), and written internal memos (Hewett et al. 2013). While generally valuable, research in this strand has limited applicability to our study for several reasons. First, it does not explore how trust is negotiated interactionally in real time but rather analyzes trust dynamics through personal testimonies and reflections "after the fact". Second, due to its socio-ethnographic focus, this research lacks explicit, micro-level linguistic analysis. Lastly, like much of the first strand, it is highly context-specific and provides few generalizable insights into the discursive dynamics and features of trust that can be readily applied to other communicative contexts.

1.4 Objectives and Research Questions

This brief overview of the literature clearly shows significant interest in the construct of trust within both forensic linguistics and discourse studies more broadly. However, we still lack a comprehensive, widely applicable framework for examining how trust is negotiated and managed in interaction. In this Element, we draw on insights from forensic linguistic research on deceptive trust building, discourse analytical work on trust, and theoretical perspectives from applied psychology and organization studies to develop such a framework. Our primary objective, therefore, is to introduce a new analytical tool that can be used to examine discursive trust management in forensic contexts and beyond. In developing this framework, we aim to take the first significant steps toward addressing the following overarching research question:

RQ1: How do speakers manage trust in interaction?

To bootstrap our model, we carry out a detailed analysis of the ETTC. Specifically, we combine 'move analysis' (Biber et al. 2007; Swales 1990; Upton & Cohen 2009) with theoretical insights from previous work on trust (see Section 2) to build a comprehensive typology of the pragmatic moves speakers use to build, maintain, and repair trust in interaction. The ETTC serves as an ideal testbed for developing our framework because, as noted earlier, Enron needed to elicit cooperation from various external stakeholders to achieve its goals, making trust a likely component of many of the recorded conversations.

The second objective of our study is to shed new light on the Enron case study itself, which will, in turn, deepen our understanding of the relationship between language, trust, and corporate corruption. As noted earlier, this is the first linguistic analysis of the ETTC. While there is extensive literature on this case study, including within forensic linguistics, where previous work has analyzed a corpus of Enron emails (Johnson & Wright 2014; Wright 2013), the role of trust and its discursive construction in enabling Enron's large-scale fraudulent activities has largely been overlooked. This leads us to our second research question:

RQ2: How did Enron traders use language to manage the trust of relevant parties in executing their illicit market manipulation?

To address this question, we draw extensively on prior detailed historical research (Nix et al. 2022), which helps us reconstruct the context and content of the conversations in the ECCT and interpret linguistic patterns. As a result, our study is thoroughly interdisciplinary, both in the development of our analytical framework and in the empirical analysis of the case study that builds upon it.

The remainder of this Element is organized as follows. Section 2 establishes the theoretical foundation of our framework by reviewing key theoretical concepts. In Section 3, we provide a historical overview of the Enron case study and additional detail about the ETTC. Section 4 outlines the methodology used in our analysis, including the procedure for annotating the corpus. Section 5 presents the analysis, beginning with a description of our typology of trust management moves. This is followed by a detailed quantitative and qualitative analysis of the ETTC, examining patterns in the frequency and use of trust management moves across different conversational contexts, move correlations and sequences, and diachronic shifts in Enron traders' discourse throughout the California energy crisis. In Section 6, we discuss the findings in relation to our two research questions. Section 7 concludes the Element with a summary of the main contributions and a brief discussion of potential avenues for future research.

2 Theoretical Background

This section reviews relevant literature outside linguistics that has informed the development of our discursive trust management framework. We begin by defining trust and discussing its core psychological and social dimensions. Next, we provide a brief overview of the phenomenon of corporate corruption, of which the Enron fraud serves as a prime example.

2.1 Trust

Trust is a fundamental element in all human relationships, underpinning cooperation, societal well-being, economic growth, and everyday interactions. As a result, it has garnered considerable attention from scholars across disciplines, giving rise to diverse definitions and theoretical perspectives (for a comprehensive overview, see Isaeva et al. 2020). Despite this variety, scholars generally agree that trust encompasses two core, interrelated components: risk and vulnerability (Rousseau et al. 1998). These aspects are effectively captured in Rousseau et al.'s (1998) widely accepted definition of trust, which forms the conceptual bedrock of our framework. The authors define trust as "a psychological state comprising the intention to accept vulnerability based upon positive expectations of the intentions or behavior of another" (Rousseau et al. 1998: 395). This definition underscores the inherent risk in trust due to the trustor's limited ability to predict or control the trustee's actions. It also emphasizes that trust is not merely a behavior or choice, but a psychological state that can lead to, or arise from, them.

If trusting others is risky and makes us vulnerable, a natural question arises: why do we choose to trust at all? Our willingness to trust others is largely shaped by our perception of their 'trustworthiness'. Trust and trustworthiness are thus two sides of the same coin. According to the influential model of interpersonal trust by Mayer et al. (1995), trustworthiness comprises three essential qualities: ability, benevolence, and integrity. Ability refers to the trustee's skills and expertise in handling the task they are entrusted with. Benevolence reflects the trustee's genuine care and positive intentions toward the trustor. Integrity has to do with moral and ethical values, that is, how honest, fair, and sincere the trustor is perceived to be. Mayer et al. (1995) propose that these three dimensions of trustworthiness are interrelated yet distinct. For instance, some individuals may be highly skilled but lack genuine care, while others may be very honest yet less competent. The relative importance of these qualities depends on the context and the nature of the relationship (Mayer & Davis 1999).

As shown in Figure 1, the Mayer et al. (1995) model suggests that, beyond our perception of a trustee's trustworthiness, our general propensity to trust others also influences our willingness to trust. Additionally, the outcomes of taking risks within a relationship affect our perceptions of the trustee, which, in turn, influence trust, creating a feedback loop. Trust is reinforced when risk-taking yields

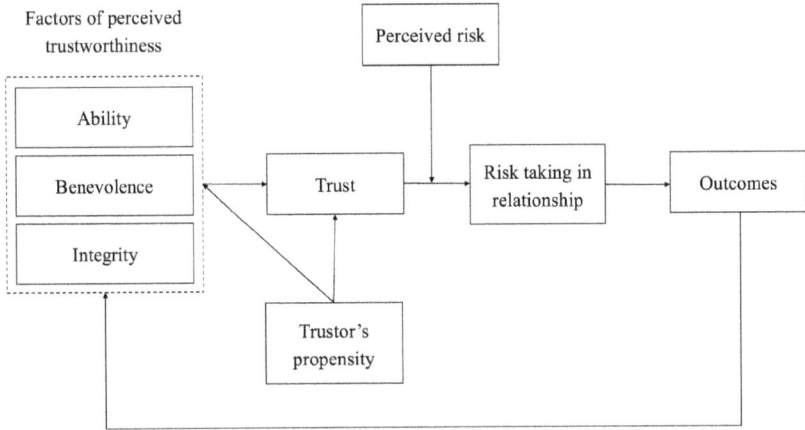

Figure 1 Mayer et al.'s model of trust (Mayer et al. 1995: 715).

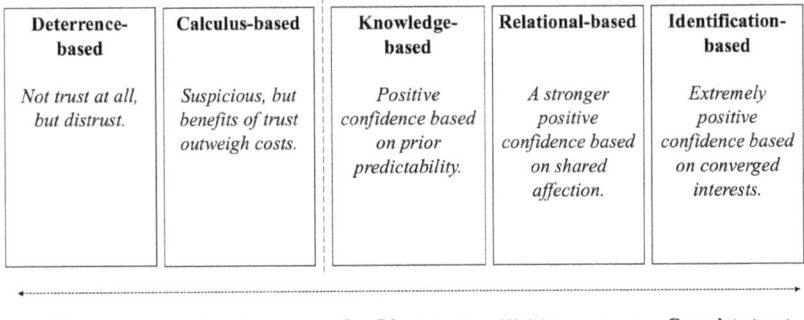

Figure 2 Different types of trust along a 'depth' continuum. Adapted from Dietz and Den Hartog (2006: 563).

expected outcomes and weakened when the trustee's behavior falls short of the trustor's positive expectations (Lewicki 2006).

The Mayer et al. (1995) model describes the general mechanisms by which trust functions in interpersonal relationships. However, relationships are not homogeneous, and they change over time as participants learn more about each other through interaction and develop a deeper interpersonal bond. Dietz and Den Hartog (2006) map different types of trust proposed in the literature along a continuum representing different degrees of depth of the trust relationship (Figure 2). On the far-left end of the continuum, 'deterrence-based' trust occurs when one party trusts another because the consequences for breaking that trust are greater than any possible gain from acting deceptively.

'Calculus-based' trust is rooted in rational choice and economic exchange. It develops when the trustor believes that the trustee will perform a beneficial action based not only on deterrence but also on credible information about the intentions or abilities of the trustee (Lewicki & Bunker 1996). 'Knowledge-based trust' relies on predictability through familiarity, rather than deterrence or rational calculation, and develops over time as a result of interactions leading to a sense of trustworthiness (Lewicki & Bunker 1996). As positive expectations are confirmed through experience, more robust forms of trust can arise, such as 'relational-based trust', which is emotional and subjective and formed from the quality of the relationship over time rather than observations of specific behaviors (Dietz & Den Hartog 2006). Finally, on the far-right end of the continuum, we find 'identification-based trust', which is established through a mutual understanding and appreciation of each other's desires and intentions (Lewicki & Bunker 1996). 'Calculus-based' and 'knowledge-based' trust are 'cognitive-based' (McAllister 1995), as they rely on rational assessments of the other person's competence, reliability, and dependability. In contrast, 'relational-based' and 'identification-based' trust are considered 'affect-based' (McAllister 1995), stemming from emotional bonds, shared experiences, and a sense of mutual care.

Another important dimension that must be considered when conceptualizing and analyzing trust is the identity of the trustee. Trust scholars have identified three main types of trust, which vary in terms of how specific the target is: 'interpersonal', 'institutional', and 'generalized' (e.g., Fulmer & Gelfand 2012; Khodyakov 2007; Spadaro et al. 2020). Interpersonal trust involves a clearly identifiable and specific target. This could be an individual, a team, or an entire organization (Fulmer & Gelfand 2012). Institutional trust refers to individuals' perceptions of significant institutions such as government, legal systems, labor unions, businesses, and organized religion (Fulmer & Gelfand 2012; Spadaro et al. 2020). With institutional trust, the target is a group or a broadly defined entity, rather than an individual with whom the person placing trust has direct personal interactions. Finally, generalized trust is the trust that individuals have in others in a society, and is based on shared norms and values. To fully understand the discursive dynamics of trust, it is important to analyze the interplay between these different trust types and their potential impact on linguistic behavior within a specific context.

Most existing literature views trust as an aspect of interpersonal relationships grounded in perceptions of the trustee's qualities (i.e., ability, benevolence, and integrity). However, social interactions also involve a more implicit form of trust that stems from a shared expectation of the predictability of social behavior and mutual understanding. This form of trust, which we shall refer to as 'situational trust', is the primary focus of Garfinkel's (1963) ethnomethodological research. According to Garfinkel (1963), trust is the expectation that others will comply with the unspoken social norms and interactional 'scripts' that govern our behavior in different social contexts. These expectations, shaped by prior experiences and culture, create a sense of normality and predictability that is essential for interpreting daily events (Garfinkel 1963: 190). When they are disrupted, trust breaks down, often leading to confusion or frustration, and requiring participants to renegotiate mutual understanding. Garfinkel (1963) demonstrated this with a series of 'breaching experiments', in which he instructed confederates to behave in ways that intentionally broke implicit social norms, such as entering a store and behaving as clerks with random customers, or responding to "How are you?" with a request for detailed clarifications like, "In what regard? My health, finances, schoolwork?".

The concept of situational trust is important to our analysis because corporate corruption is a context-dependent phenomenon that emerges dynamically from interactions between participants. In such relationships, the clandestine nature of corrupt activities makes it challenging for corrupt individuals to establish a stable basis for anticipating the behavior of others involved. This underscores the pivotal role of verbal interaction as a site where the "rules" of corrupt cooperation are jointly established by participants, leading to the emergence of situational trust. Thus, both situational and interpersonal trust are cornerstones of corrupt networks. Participants must build mutual understanding of their illicit ties while projecting trustworthiness to ensure the network's survival and growth. More broadly, situational and interpersonal trust are best understood as interdependent dimensions. For example, unpredictable or unexpected behavior may lead to a breakdown of situational trust, which in turn is likely to prompt a re-evaluation of both the situation and the trustee, potentially calling their ability and integrity into question.

Finally, it is important to recognize that trust is not static; it is a constantly evolving aspect of relationships, shaped by both material actions and communication (e.g., Cook 2001; Marková & Gillespie 2008; Mayer et al. 1995). Trust can be undermined by behaviors that contradict expectations about the trustee or the situation, leading to a reassessment of the relationship and the trustee's ability, benevolence, and integrity (Lewicki 2006). To rebuild trust and preserve the relationship, the individual who breached it may work to enhance their perceived trustworthiness and reestablish consistency and predictability in their interactions. Trust can be restored not only by modifying one's behavior but also through discourse. Accordingly, our analysis seeks to identify not only the discursive strategies Enron traders used to build trust with their interlocutors but also the verbal tactics they employed to repair trust when external events or statements during conversations undermined it.

2.2 Corporate Corruption

As a concept, corruption captures the misuse of power for personal or collective gain (Ashforth et al. 2008). It can occur in various social contexts and is not limited to explicit legal violations. Instead, it focuses on the deviation from accepted social norms, misappropriation of entrusted positions, and actions taken for undue benefit. In organizations, corruption can be used for the benefit of the organization or individuals within it and is often collectively practiced and enacted as part of 'normal' business functions and operations (Palmer 2012; Pinto et al. 2008). Examples of such corrupt behaviors in a corporate context include illicit transactions (e.g., bribery), agreements (e.g., price-fixing), deception (e.g., misleading investors), or manipulative practices (e.g., market abuse).

While such behaviors have a long history, corporate corruption scandals have become increasingly common in the recent past, driven in part by ambiguous regulations and a focus on entrepreneurial innovation (Balleisen 2018). This was evident in the US savings and loan industry, where deregulation led to widespread fraudulent practices (Black et al. 1995). Similarly, the globalization and deregulation of the 1980s have been associated with a rise in corporate illegality and corruption, as the emphasis on financial innovation and global competitiveness blurred established business norms and heightened expectations for exceptional performance (Goldfarb & Kirsch 2019).

Within organizations, certain characteristics, such as culture and leadership style, and organizational structures like incentives, can encourage corruption. In such cases, corruption can be seen as a viable means of achieving an aggressive target within an ethical climate that focuses on outcome over approach. In particular, the process of normalization shows how the actions of a few individuals can become widespread and routine as they are incorporated into the organization's structures and processes (Ashforth & Anand 2003; Palmer 2008). Even when wrongdoers are aware of the transgressive nature of their actions, they may use alternative interpretations to justify them and reframe dissonant information in line with a morally acceptable explanation (Ariely 2012). Incumbent perpetrators may also use these rationalizations to socialize newcomers into the group's particularistic worldview, which sees corrupt acts as legitimate.

While the reasons behind corruption have been widely studied, there are fewer studies on the specifics of how it is carried out and managed within organizations. Thus, while we have a general understanding of what causes organizations to engage in corrupt acts, we know little about how it is planned, executed, and coordinated. Additionally, the complex role of external actors in corruption is not well understood. While acts like bribery or price-fixing clearly involve external parties, it is possible that other, less overly transactional forms of corruption extend beyond a single organization. In this regard, previous research on Enron has shown that the relationship between corrupt organizations and the unwitting or conscious involvement of clients can form a key context for 'network-enabled' corruption (Nix et al. 2022). This study seeks to deepen our understanding of how relationships contribute to corruption by re-examining Enron's manipulation of California's energy markets, focusing on how trust between Enron traders and their contacts (clients and regulators) enabled corruption as an organizational phenomenon.

Corruption often involves the breaking of laws, but it can also extend beyond the technically illegal to include wrongful activities that are judged to transgress broader social norms. Therefore, while lawfulness is often an important consideration, it is not a defining criterion. This is an important consideration, especially when considering past cases, as legal proceedings are influenced by social, financial, and political conditions, as well as the available evidence (Grieve et al. 2010). However, it is widely recognized that Enron's actions in California, discussed in more detail in Section 3, deviated from acceptable social norms, both in terms of ethical standards and the law. Indeed, this is a well-established case of wrongdoing, which therefore provides an ideal starting point for exploring how corporate corruption was carried out over time within an organizational division and through its interactions with other market participants, and for advancing our understanding of the phenomenon of corporate corruption and the discursive dynamics of trust underpinning it.

3 The Enron Case Study

This section provides an overview of the Enron case study and our data. We begin with a brief historical summary of California's energy market deregulation, which set the stage for Enron's fraud. Next, we outline the market manipulation strategies employed by Enron traders to exploit vulnerabilities in the newly deregulated market. We then introduce the Enron Trader Tapes Corpus and explain how it was compiled. We conclude the section with a brief discussion of the main limitations of this corpus.

3.1 Californian Energy Deregulation as a Context for Corruption

Grid systems supply electricity via three key components: generation, transmission, and distribution. Generation produces electricity at facilities like natural gas power stations or hydroelectric dams. Transmission transfers this at a high voltage using pylons and cables. Distribution then delivers power directly to homes and businesses via substations, low-voltage lines, and underground cables. Within the US, these functions were historically managed by vertically integrated utilities, which controlled the entire process – from generation to distribution – within a defined region. Accordingly, California's pre-1998 electricity industry represented an integrated model of energy supply, which was dominated by large utilities with no direct competition.

The fact that energy is fundamentally transient in nature complicates the process of its large-scale provision, as electricity needs to be used at the same time as it is generated. Excess electricity overloads infrastructure, while shortages lead to brownouts or blackouts, making precise real-time supply and demand balancing essential. To make this more feasible within large continental areas like North America, regional interconnections allow states to manage local systems and exchange power regionally, ensuring stable operations (Figure 3). Regional grids also rely on forward planning, real-time adjustments, and contingency reserves. This 'scheduling' process organizes energy generation and transmission in advance, anticipating availability and demand. Care is taken to avoid transmission congestion by minimizing imbalances in energy

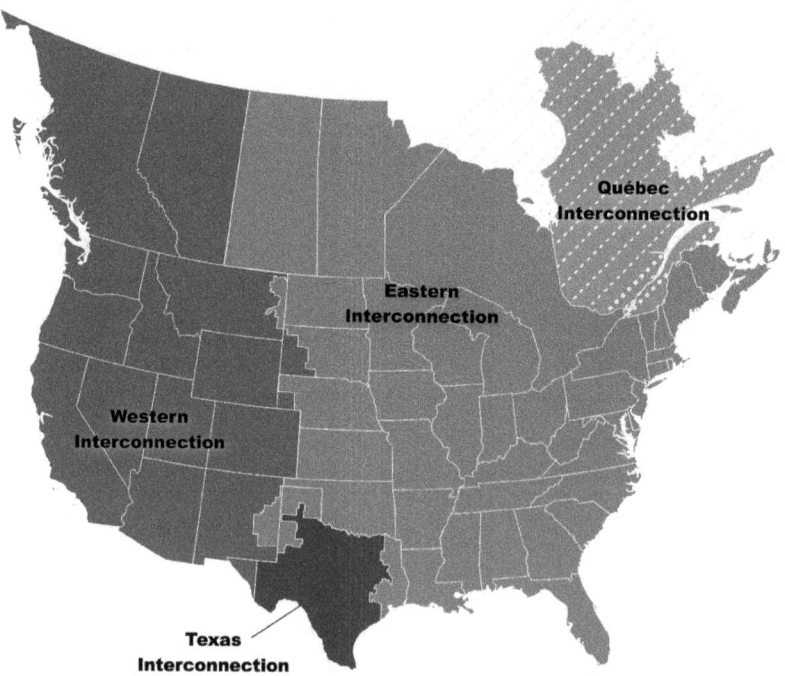

Figure 3 Map of US energy interconnections.

flows (e.g., north to south). Close to the scheduled time, adjustments refine supply, and reserves address unexpected shortfalls.

By the late 1980s, however, California faced several energy-related challenges, including high electricity prices (30–50% above the national average) and stalled new generation projects (Blumstein et al. 2002). Inspired by successful natural gas reforms (Bhagwat 2003), the state looked to greater competition, and on 23rd September 1996, after consultation and planning phases beginning in 1992, it initiated the first deregulated electricity system in the US. Ultimately, the legislation enacting this restructuring aimed to induce competition, lower consumer prices, and improve reliability by breaking up the integrated model of energy supply.

Under the new system, represented schematically in Figure 4, consumers were no longer captive and could choose their provider. Additionally, consumer rates were reduced and capped for the first few years of the new system's operation. Importantly, utilities were required to sell and purchase power on a newly created spot market run by the California Power Exchange (PX). Even where they had their own generation capacity to do so, utilities were required to use the market to purchase all the energy needed to serve their consumers. In promoting the use of the PX market, the regulations also curtailed their ability to enter into long-term supply deals directly with other parties (i.e., bilateral contracts), making the PX markets the main mechanism for selling and acquiring electricity.

While the PX had a chiefly financial function, the newly created California Independent Systems Operator (ISO) would manage the physical delivery of

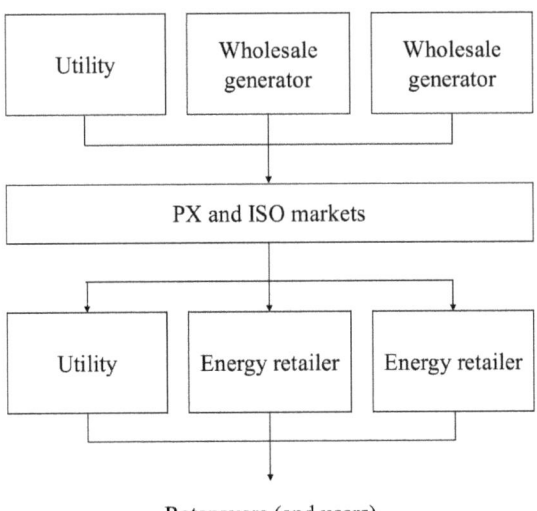

Figure 4 Deregulated market structure (adapted from Weare 2003: 11).

electricity. Utilities, which historically owned transmission lines, were required to transfer operational control of them to the ISO. This allowed the ISO to manage the market activity of the PX through centralized control of state transmission. As part of this, the ISO was also responsible for managing contingency and adjustment administration (i.e., balancing the grid), something it did largely through an automated computer system. As such, the ISO would receive the PX's market information, and its system would then set about ensuring there was enough power to support the anticipated demand. If a line was congested, artificial price adjustments in the form of congestion relief payments would be used to incentivize the required change in scheduled flow. In this way, the ISO's role in the new structure would be to convert energy as a financial commodity into the physical movement of electricity.

For nearly two years, this deregulated energy system functioned broadly as anticipated. However, by 2000, extreme weather, limited infrastructure, and what would transpire to be corrupt trading practices created a severe energy supply shortage and massively inflated wholesale prices (Blumstein et al. 2002). The resulting energy crisis led to rolling blackouts, organizational bankruptcies, and significant public costs. The FERC would later reveal that Texas-based energy company Enron was among those that had manipulated California's energy markets, gaining enormous profits while exacerbating the financial, infrastructural, and political turmoil (FERC 2003b, 2007). Table 1 summarizes the key crisis events chronologically. The next section expands on Enron's market manipulation practices.

Table 1 Summary of events relating to Enron and the California energy crisis.

Date	Event
July 1997	Enron (primarily a Texas-based natural gas company) acquires Portland General Electric, allowing them to operate within the Western Interconnection and thus California's impending electricity markets.
April 1998	California's deregulated electricity system begins operations.
May 2000	After two years, unusual price increases appear. Due to caps on consumer prices, California's utilities cannot pass on the increased costs.
June 2000	Rolling blackouts occur in northern California as reserve energy falls below required levels. California's energy markets (the ISO and PX) reach highs.

Table 1 (cont.)

Date	Event
December 2000	Having investigated the summer's energy price issues, the FERC allows wholesale prices above the cap to encourage energy supply.
April 2001	The FERC requires utility companies with spare energy to offer it to California's markets.
June 2001	The crisis subsides and energy prices return to pre-crisis levels.
December 2001	Enron files for bankruptcy. Allegations that it manipulated energy markets throughout the western States intensify.
February 2002	The FERC orders an investigation of Enron and other sellers during the crisis.

3.2 Enron's Manipulation of California's Energy Markets

Originating ostensibly as a gas company, Enron was known in the 1990s for its innovative financial and performance-driven culture. Indeed, California's deregulation aligned with an organizational climate focused on free market ideals and profit maximization (Benke 2018) and followed years of industry lobbying for such reforms. Once implemented, Enron quickly secured an operational base on the West Coast, acquiring Portland General Electric (PGE) in July 1997. In contrast to PGE, which operated as a utility company with generation and distribution obligations, the newly created West Power division would engage solely in wholesale energy trading and scheduling, primarily on behalf of third-party clients (e.g., other utilities). Indeed, the legal requirement to keep the two companies separate emphasized the trading division's interest in electricity as a purely financial commodity and the understanding that they did not control electricity infrastructure or operations.

From inception, West Power's senior traders studied the new system's rules and protocols to prepare for California's deregulation, identifying several design flaws that presented lucrative opportunities for exploitation. By late 1997, traders were already actively probing the market's weaknesses, and by late 1999, they had formalized this knowledge into a set of 'trading strategies' that exploited California's system while masking their true intent (see Table 2). These strategies represented repeatable scheduling and transaction patterns that, once routinized and embedded in the division's operations, allowed Enron's traders to systematically exploit the new markets' weaknesses. Over time, these

Table 2 Summary of Enron's key trading strategies based on de Bruijne (2009).

Type	Trading strategies	Description
Prohibited arbitrage	Export of Californian power	Exporting energy from California and selling to more lucrative out-of-state markets (without a price cap).
	Ricochet (a.k.a Megawatt Laundering)	Exporting energy out of the ISO's system, thus avoiding price caps and decreasing supply. Then re-importing to sell in the next day's real-time markets.
	Fat Boy	Falsely overscheduling load in the hour or day-ahead markets and selling surplus in the higher real-time markets.
	Thin Man	Falsely under-scheduling load in the hour or day-ahead markets and then buying cheaper energy in the real-time markets.
Congestion-based	Death Star (variations included Forney's Perpetual Loop and Driscoll's Death Star)	Scheduling fictitious transmission in a loop that flows in the opposite direction to a congested path, thus collecting congestion relief revenues.
	Load Shift	Scheduling large demand for energy in order to change the market price and then buy or sell in that market at a higher return.
	Wheel-Out	Purposefully scheduling transmission on a path that is out of service to obtain congestion revenues.
	Non-firm Export	Scheduling non-firm energy for export on a congested line with no intention or ability to deliver. Congestion revenues collected.

Table 2 (cont.)

Type	Trading strategies	Description
	Scheduling to collect congestion charges	Scheduling energy in order to congest a path, then receiving a payment to cancel the schedule, thus relieving the congestion.
Ancillary services-based (reserve power)	Get Shorty (a.k.a Paper Trading)	Selling reserves in the day-ahead markets and then buying them in the cheaper real-time market.
	Selling non-firm energy as firm	Fraudulently labelling energy as firm (backed-up by reserve power), when in fact it is non-firm.
	Double selling	Selling the same reserve power to multiple markets, i.e., as day-ahead reserves and then again in real-time trading.

strategies spread beyond individual traders to become a normalized part of the collective activity within the division, even forming part of the formal training and assessment requirements.

While Enron's strategies were primarily enacted among its own traders, they relied on partnerships with external organizations. In particular, many strategies required transmission paths or generation assets located across the Western Interconnection. For example, the 'Ricochet' strategy involved exporting energy on paper to disguise it as 'out-of-state', then reselling it at inflated prices in the next day's real-time market. This depended on the external cooperation afforded to Enron via their role as a trusted financial agent, which provided access to operational decision-making and information and created the illusion of legitimate trading while actually enabling manipulation. In addition to infrastructure access, Enron traders also leveraged their consultancy relationships with external companies. Through informal profit-sharing agreements, presented to clients as legitimate market tactics, these partnerships gave Enron control over scheduling and trading activities, facilitating the execution of manipulation strategies. Such arrangements converted theoretical opportunities into practical, repeatable practices.

Despite their widespread use and the fact that many parties entered them in good faith, these partnerships often also violated market rules designed to limit the market power of intermediary firms like Enron. The earliest of these partnerships was with Texas-based utility El Paso Electric, which Enron traders used to create schedules that appeared to legitimately generate congestion relief revenues without physically moving energy or taking on risk (Forney 2000). Additionally, Enron assumed control over much of El Paso's scheduling activity, using privileged information to manipulate generation units for trading purposes. This relationship provided early proof of concept for Enron's manipulation strategies, with the El Paso arrangements serving as a model for similar relationships with other organizations (SNOPUD 2007).

As this suggests, Enron's actions were embedded within a complex inter-organizational network that materially enabled its corruption (Nix et al. 2022). While actual awareness of Enron's practices and motives appears to have varied dramatically, these external partnerships allowed its traders to pursue shared profitability, as clients ceded control of physical assets, provided market information, and devolved operational decision-making to the firm. Much of this activity was coordinated via telephone, providing trace insights into the mechanisms through which trust and cooperation were established. In particular, forensic evidence from the FERC investigation offers access to recordings of conversations between Enron traders as well as with their external partners (i.e. the ETTC). These reveal the discursive strategies underpinning the development of trust and cooperation among the actors involved. By analyzing these interactions, we gain a clearer understanding of how networks used for corruption emerge and function in practice. Enron's ability to operationalize its manipulation strategies rested not only on its internal organizational culture but also on these external relationships, which extended the reach and scale of its activities.

In sum, Enron's exploitation of California's deregulated energy market was not an isolated phenomenon but the product of its traders' systemic and networked control of industry infrastructure and operational decision-making. The firm's West Power division, driven by an aggressive profit-maximizing ethos, capitalized on design flaws in California's energy system. Through repeatable trading strategies, its use of partnerships with external organizations, and the operationalization of market manipulation as a routine practice, Enron was able to realize extreme returns for both itself and its clients. The crisis that followed revealed not only the fragility and flaws of California's deregulated market but also the extent of Enron's influence.

3.3 The Enron Trader Tapes Corpus

The ETTC includes typed transcripts from digital audio recordings of 505 internal and external telephone conversations involving Enron employees in the period surrounding the California energy crisis. External recipients of these calls include other companies colluding with Enron, companies that were unwitting participants or even victims of Enron's actions, members of Enron's broader organizational structure, and independent entities responsible for managing the sale and supply of electricity across California, namely the ISO and the PX. The original transcripts, sourced from the FERC library (https://elibrary.ferc.gov/eLibrary/search), required substantial pre-processing to create an analyzable corpus. Specifically, they were released as non-searchable PDFs of original court files and thus had to be converted into plain text format, a task we outsourced to a company specializing in audio transcription services. Additionally, as almost half of the files included multiple conversations, they had to be split to ensure each represented a single interaction. We also removed boilerplate text and irrelevant headers/footers and applied a file-naming scheme that includes the date of the transcript, its original document ID number, the caller names, and conversation-level codes (see Section 4.4). We have made the fully digitized, pre-processed corpus available via the Open Science Framework (OSF) repository at the following URL: https://osf.io/ngdhx/.

Table 3 summarizes the corpus details. The corpus covers the period from January 2000 to January 2002. However, these calls only represent a fraction of those that took place over this period. The tapes themselves exist because trading floor desks at Enron West Power had recorded phone lines to monitor oral offers and acceptance of deals. However, these were not routinely transcribed, and it was only after the California energy crisis, when the tapes were used in evidence, that transcriptions were produced. Given the cost implications, only those conversations of potential relevance to the case were transcribed. This results in some notable gaps and bunching within the corpus, as Figure 5 shows.

Although not originally intended for detailed linguistic analysis, the transcripts in the ETTC are of high quality. In addition to the content of the utterances, they

Table 3 Enron Trader Tapes Corpus details.

Time frame covered	29.01.2000–10.01.2002
Number of files	505
Average conversation length	829.9 words ($SD = 1147.8$ words)
Total size	414,964 words

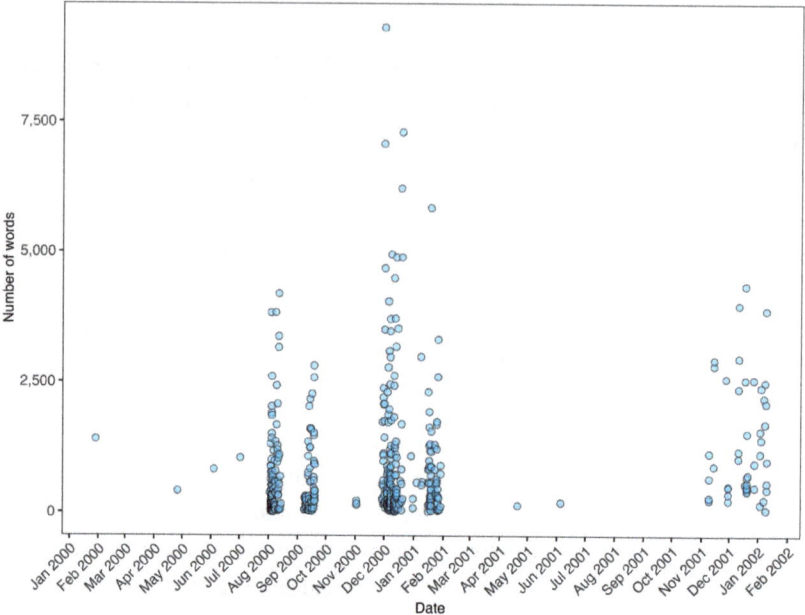

Figure 5 Diachronic distribution and length of conversations in the Enron Trader Tapes Corpus.

capture some paralinguistic features, including various vocalizations like laughter, coughing, throat clearing, and pause fillers such as "uhm," "ah," and "um". Notably, transcribers have refrained from "sanitizing" the calls based on normative standards, a practice commonly observed in corpora originally designed for institutional purposes rather than linguistic analysis like the Hansard corpus of parliamentary discourse (Mollin 2007). The transcripts retain non-standard grammatical constructions (e.g., "*I don't got* a problem with goin'") and various kinds of disfluencies such as truncated words and intonation units (e.g., "So write down, *please-* write down the *hum* – the time and *the* – your Turret ID and all that."). Speech overlaps are not recorded systematically; in-text annotations (e.g., "simultaneous speaking") are used to indicate overlapping speech, without, however, specifying which portions of the speakers' turns are overlapping. Pauses are not consistently recorded either. Long pauses are sometimes annotated in-text (e.g., "Um, [pause] yeah, bought uh, they bought -"). Shorter pauses are not recorded. Instances of 'latching', where a speaker begins a new turn while the previous speaker's turn is still ongoing, are often marked with a dash. Punctuation marks appear to be used to capture prosodic information, with the full stop, comma, and question mark symbols indicating 'terminative', 'continuative', and 'appeal' contours, respectively (Du Bois et al. 1993). However, it is not possible to verify

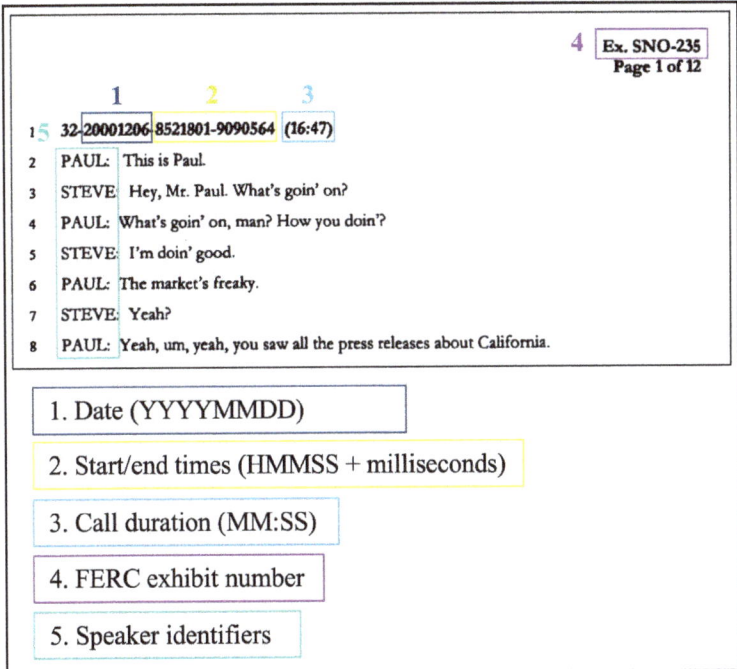

Figure 6 Encoding of contextual information in the original FERC files.

this conclusively or to assess the accuracy of the other interactional and prosodic features mentioned above because we do not have sufficient access to the original audio files or the transcription protocols used. However, as our analysis primarily focuses on the content of the conversations, this does not pose a significant issue.

Apart from capturing the context and paralinguistic features of the calls, the transcripts released by FERC provide various contextual details, such as the date and duration of the call, and information about the speakers, as illustrated in Figure 6. This contextual information is useful for situating the calls, interpretating their content, and grouping them to compare linguistic patterns across interactional contexts.

3.4 Data Limitations

The principal limitation we faced in interpreting the ETTC stems from its creation circumstances. While telephone recordings at Enron were largely preserved through formal data and records of management processes, the corpus should not be considered complete or exhaustive. Firstly, as noted above, not all phone calls were recorded or preserved, and such absences are most evident during the latter crisis period, when communication practices shifted to more secure channels, such as cell phones (Nix et al. 2022). Thus, we must assume that Enron's awareness of potential incrimination meant that some interactions relevant to the study were likely never recorded. Selective transcription and publication further reduced the size and composition of the corpus, as the transcriptions submitted to the FERC as evidence represent only a fraction of the available telecommunications data. Naturally, as these transcripts were intended to support the case against Enron, they focus exclusively on interactions deemed relevant to demonstrating traders' manipulation of the energy markets (Pechman 2005). As a result, the corpus reflects a relevant but selective sample and is not qualitatively or quantitatively representative of all trading-floor communication within Enron at that time. This selective focus also limits our ability to identify diachronic trends at a fine-grained level and draw definitive conclusions about the development of specific trust relationships over time.

Another challenge lies in the highly contextualized nature of the data. Naturally occurring conversations often build on participants' shared background knowledge and tacit understanding, leaving many elements that would aid third-party interpretation implicit. This is particularly true of the short, high-frequency interactions that characterized many of the trading calls within the corpus. In some cases, a lack of context resulted in ambiguities regarding the specific relational context, intended meaning, or the practical implications of interactions. This was particularly true for external speakers as their identity was not automatically recorded. Such challenges are familiar in historical research, which frequently deals with partial and incomplete sources that require triangulation and researcher inference.

Given the critical role of context in this linguistic study, we explicitly integrate a historical element into our analysis. That is, our work builds on prior historical research into Enron's role in the California energy crisis (Nix et al. 2022), and the analytical process included routine cross-checks between linguistic interpretations and historical accounts of the crisis and the specific telephone interactions under study. This historical and contextually situated approach to linguistic analysis ensured that our analysis maintained dual integrity (Maclean et al. 2016) between our theoretical interests and the empirical setting from which we derived our findings.

4 Methodology

As outlined in the introduction, previous research lacks a broadly applicable framework for analyzing how speakers use language to manage trust in conversation. To address this gap and examine how Enron traders discursively negotiated trust with relevant parties while manipulating California's energy markets, we developed our own framework. At its heart is a typology of 'trust management moves', which we developed by complementing the well-established method of move analysis with insights from trust theory. This typology provides a comprehensive inventory of the discursive strategies available to speakers to negotiate and manage trust in interaction. This section presents our typology and describes the procedure we followed to identify and annotate the moves in the ETTC.

4.1 Move Analysis

Move analysis is a widely used discourse analytical technique for identifying the functional components that structure communication, whether in spoken or written genres. This approach posits that communication achieves its purpose through a series of distinct yet complementary verbal actions, known as 'moves'. For example, a research article introduction typically includes moves like 'establishing a territory', 'establishing a niche', and 'occupying the niche' to persuade the reader of the study's relevance and position it within the existing field of research (Swales 1990). Moves have identifiable linguistic boundaries and typically follow a predictable sequence that reflects the rhetorical structure and purpose of the genre (Biber et al. 2007). For instance, business emails typically begin with a greeting (e.g., "Dear Team"), followed by an opening move that establishes the purpose of the email (e.g., "I'm reaching out to discuss our project timeline"), then provide relevant details or requests (e.g., "Please review the attached schedule and confirm your availability"), and conclude with a closing formula (e.g., "Thank you for your attention to this matter"). As function-based units, moves vary in length but generally include at least one proposition (Biber et al. 2007). They can often be broken down into more specific elements, referred to as 'steps' (Swales 1990) or 'strategies' (Bhatia 1993). For example, the 'establishing a territory' move in academic articles is typically made up of the more specific steps of 'claiming centrality', 'making topic generalizations', and 'reviewing items of previous research' (Swales 1990). By deconstructing communication into these functional elements, move analysis enables researchers to uncover the underlying strategies that guide how a text or conversation accomplishes its goals within a particular communicative situation.

Move analysis was originally developed to identify typical patterns of discourse organization within specific genres, such as academic research articles or business reports. The primary aim of this approach is to uncover implicit textual conventions that shape communication in particular contexts. This often involves distinguishing between 'obligatory' and 'optional' moves, examining how moves combine to form predictable sequences, and exploring how genre structures evolve over time in response to societal, institutional, and communicative changes (e.g., Groom & Grieve 2019). However, move analysis can also serve as a more general descriptive tool to identify significant, recurring verbal actions that fulfill specific purposes within a discourse, without necessarily focusing on defining a genre. An example of this more flexible approach in forensic linguistics is Chiang et al. (2020), who use move analysis to explore the linguistic behavior of suspected child sexual offenders on the dark web, aiming to identify patterns that distinguish different types of users (e.g., authority figures vs other users) rather than describing the genre of "dark web image exchange interactions". In our study, we take a similar approach. Our goal is to begin uncovering the pragmatics of trust rather than characterizing the genre of "energy trading telephone conversations".

4.2 Framework Development

We developed our framework progressively across three main stages. To bootstrap our typology of trust management moves, Fuoli and Nix first conducted a pilot qualitative analysis of twelve transcripts from our corpus. Guided by previous historical analysis of the Enron case (Nix et al. 2022), we selected transcripts in which trust was likely to be a central issue, offering a productive starting point to identify linguistic features related to it.

The move analysis process was both "top-down" and "bottom-up": as we read the texts, we looked for instances of moves previously identified in forensic linguistic studies on deceptive trust manipulation and discourse analytical research on trust, such as 'praise' and 'deny', while also searching for previously undocumented moves that, based on trust theory and our analysis of the conversation, appeared to serve a trust management function. For a move to be included in our taxonomy, we needed to be able to clearly and explicitly articulate (1) how it relates to and potentially influences trust, and (2) which of the three facets of trustworthiness from Mayer et al.'s (1995) model it could help enhance. This information was organized into a codebook that, for each move, also included a corpus example and specific coding guidelines. Table 4 shows an example of a move specification from the codebook.

Our analysis was also informed by research in pragmatics and discourse analysis on the related phenomena of 'rapport management' (Spencer-Oatey 2008) and 'politeness' (Brown & Levinson 1987). We included in our typology moves that, beyond their politeness and rapport-building functions, may also serve to manage trust. For example, the move we term 'keep option open' builds trust by signaling the speaker's adaptability and benevolent intentions. At the same time, from a politeness perspective, this move can be described as

Table 4 Example of specification for the trust management move 'signal confidentiality'.

Function	Relationship to trust	Facets of trustworthiness at play	Corpus example	Code-specific guidelines
To designate a statement or information shared in a conversation as confidential, secret, and intended for private discussion without disclosure to others.	By explicitly designating the shared content as confidential, we not only demonstrate our trust in the other person to maintain secrecy but also foster a stronger connection and alignment between us and our conversation partner.	Integrity	A: Yeah, and I – she's re – really, really upset with us, and you see, the way this works out is we're an SC for somebody and – B: Right. A: – this – this m– you know in between me and you B: Mm hm. A: Unofficially, I guess. B: Right.	This move should not be mixed with the 'share privileged information' move. The latter refers to the content of the utterance, which, based on the context, may be inferred as morally or legally problematic. The 'signal confidentiality' move is limited to expressions that serve to explicitly frame what is said as confidential.

performing 'negative politeness' (Brown & Levinson 1987). This initial exploratory analysis led to a tentative list of seventeen trust management moves.

In Stage 2, Fuoli and Wickert applied the initial set of moves to a sample of forty-five conversations from the corpus that included the initial twelve plus thirty-three new conversations. Using the annotation program Nvivo (QSR International 2022), we coded these texts independently in three roughly equal batches, then met to compare annotations. Through discussion, we identified areas for improvement within the framework. Two of the initial moves were merged with others for parsimony, and six new move categories were added to capture trust management strategies not covered by the original set. Where needed, we refined category labels and moved descriptions to enhance clarity and precision. The codebook was progressively expanded with new examples and move-specific guidelines to improve the consistency and replicability of our approach. By the end of this collaborative coding phase, we had established a stable set of twenty-one moves, ready for application to the rest of the corpus.

In the third and final stage, we applied the typology to the remaining 465 conversations in the corpus. While major revisions to the typology and codebook occurred during the second stage, minor adjustments were also implemented in this final stage, particularly regarding the labeling of move categories and move-specific guidelines in the codebook. Following any adjustments, we updated all previous annotations to align them with the revised codebook. The final, consolidated typology of trust management moves is presented in more detail in Section 5.1. The codebook is available via our OSF repository.

4.3 Annotation Procedure and Reliability Assessment

As part of Stage 2 of the framework development process, we also assessed the reliability of our annotation guidelines. We calculated inter-coder agreement scores for each of the three batches of transcripts independently coded by Fuoli and Wickert. Following Fuoli (2018a) and acknowledging the inherent challenges in achieving perfect reliability in interpretive discourse analysis, we view reliability testing primarily as a reflexive procedure aimed at strengthening the coding protocol and making it as robust and transparent as possible. After each batch of independent coding, we thoroughly reviewed discrepancies and collaboratively refined the coding guidelines to address sources of disagreement. In addition to revising the typology of trust management moves, we added general guidelines on practical aspects of annotation, such as segmenting units and handling disfluencies.

Across the three rounds of coding, we achieved an average inter-coder agreement of 81.52%, which indicates that our coding procedure is fairly reliable. However, we did not observe an improvement in the level of agreement across the three rounds of coding, despite our best efforts to refine the coding guidelines (round 1: 85.83%; round 2: 78.92%; round 3: 79.80%). This is likely due to a combination of factors. The abundance of technical jargon in the transcripts made the annotation task incredibly demanding, as annotators had to simultaneously decipher the content and identify trust management moves. The frequent speech disfluencies further complicated this process. As a result, many straightforward instances were missed simply due to fatigue or concentration lapses, as we discovered when comparing our coding. Moreover, each new batch of data brought unique, unexpected challenges.

Given the solid but less-than-perfect agreement scores and the challenges in achieving consistent improvements, we decided to complete the coding of the rest of the corpus collaboratively. This strategy improves the quality of the annotation because it promotes cooperative rather than idiosyncratic coding strategies, and because the annotators are forced to make their reasoning explicit and convince each other in case of disagreement (Spooren & Degand 2010). The obvious drawback of this strategy, however, is that it is very time-consuming.

Fuoli and Wickert divided the remaining corpus equally and annotated their respective portions independently. Upon completion, they met to discuss any issues, challenges, and potential further modifications to the framework and codebook. Next, they checked each other's batches and suggested edits to the coding where necessary. Once the cross-checking was complete, Fuoli and Wickert reviewed and reconciled any remaining coding discrepancies. The full corpus annotation process took approximately 9 months and required an estimated ~1,300 person-hours. In the interest of transparency and replicability, we have made the Nvivo file containing the fully annotated corpus available via our OSF repository.

4.4 Conversation-Level Codes

In addition to performing in-text annotations, we coded conversations in the ETTC according to three situational criteria: participants, nature of the call, and nature of the tie between participants. These conversation-level codes were designed to facilitate comparisons across different communicative tasks and situations. Our goal was to identify patterns, explore how external factors influence trust management, and gain a nuanced understanding of Enron's strategies during the crisis. This comparison also serves as a "sanity check"

Table 5 Conversation-level codes.

Participants	Internal
	External
	Unknown
Nature of the call	Client-agent
	Trading/scheduling
	Coordination
	Regulatory/rules
	Social
	Other
Nature of the tie	New contact
	Known/formal
	Known/informal
	Close

for our model. For example, we anticipate differences in trust behavior between internal calls with a social purpose and formal conversations between Enron and regulators.

Table 5 outlines the conversation-level codes and sub-categories we applied to the transcripts. The 'participants' code distinguishes between internal Enron calls and external calls involving Enron employees and individuals from other organizations. Speaker information was obtained from FERC-released documentation and extensive prior research on this case study conducted by Nix and colleagues (Nix et al. 2022; Nix & Decker 2023).

The 'nature of the call' category broadly captures the call's purpose, providing important context for analyzing trust-management discourse. It has six sub-categories. 'Client-agent' refers to calls where Enron staff manage their relationships with client companies or offer them advice on market trends and trading strategy. The 'trading/scheduling' category includes calls focused on specific trading transactions or the creation of schedules for energy delivery. 'Coordination' covers calls where Enron's traders made logistical arrangements, which were often associated with controlling or manipulating energy flows. These calls occur either between Enron and external parties (e.g., coordinating power generator usage with a client) or internally within Enron (e.g., planning energy schedules and market moves). 'Regulatory/rules' encompasses calls where participants discuss the rules and regulations governing the California energy markets. These conversations might involve direct interaction with the market operators (ISO and PX) or discussions within Enron's legal and public relations teams. 'Social' identifies calls containing substantial amounts of casual discourse, such as chatting, gossiping, storytelling, or joking. Finally, 'other' is used for calls that do not clearly fit into any of the above categories.

The 'nature of the tie' code categorizes the quality of the relationship between callers, indicating how personal, close, or familiar it is. Some conversations in the corpus are rather formal or clearly involve people who do not know each other well. Others indicate close and often frequent interaction between participants, even if just in a professional context. As external information regarding the nature of participant relationships was limited, we often had to rely on qualitative analysis of the transcripts, aided by known historical factors like participants' roles in Enron's activities and the frequency of their interactions in the corpus. Key interactional and linguistic indicators we considered to infer the degree of intimacy between participants included deviations from task-oriented content (social chat, gossip, opinions), informal language use (swearing, nicknames, slang), and the presence of joking, laughter, or sarcasm.

These detailed guidelines used for conversation-level codes are accessible through our OSF repository. To assess their reliability, Fuoli and Nix conducted three rounds of inter-coder agreement testing using the same dataset as for the in-text annotations tests. The results showed very robust agreement in all the categories, with 97.22%, 91.16%, and 96.97% agreement for 'participants', 'nature of the call', and 'nature of the tie' respectively, and a grand average of 95.12%. Given the strength of these results, we decided that the rest of the conversations could be categorized by a single person. Fuoli completed this part of the work. Conversations that were difficult to categorize were submitted to Nix for advice. We also conducted extensive checks for the 'nature of the tie' category to ensure that in cases where the same participants appeared in multiple calls, their relationship had been categorized consistently.

5 Trust Management in the Enron Trader Tapes Corpus

In this section, we present the results of our analysis. We begin by outlining our typology of trust management moves before examining how Enron traders employed them. The analysis starts with a quantitative overview of the moves' distribution, followed in Section 5.3 by a qualitative analysis of key extracts that illustrate their use in various contexts and their role in Enron's broader trust management strategy. Section 5.4 explores how the identity of the interlocutor, the depth of the relationship with them, and the overall purpose of the conversation shaped Enron traders' discourse. In Section 5.5, we analyze quantitative correlations between the moves to identify sequential patterns of discursive trust management. The section concludes with an exploration of diachronic trends in the use of the moves throughout the California energy crisis. The section includes several abridged extracts from the corpus. Full conversations and annotations are available via our OSF repository. We encourage readers to consult these resources for additional detail and to follow our analysis with greater ease.

Before we delve into the analysis, an important clarification is warranted. This analysis focuses on Enron's role as a known perpetrator of market manipulation and gaming during the California energy crisis. While it has been established that Enron's relationships with clients and transactional partners outside the organization were integral to its actions, the nature of these relationships varied widely, encompassing different formal and informal arrangements and differing levels of awareness regarding Enron's strategies and their broader implications for energy markets. It is not the aim of this study to make assumptions or claims about the intentions or culpability of any external parties associated with Enron or represented in our findings. Moreover, we do not equate partnership with Enron or trust in its traders as synonymous with collusion and recognize that many individuals and organizations represented in the ETTC were not complicit in, or aware of, Enron's misconduct.

5.1 Typology of Trust Management Moves

Table 6 outlines the twenty-one trust management moves in our typology alongside short corpus examples. Move definitions and further details on how each move relates to trust are provided in the codebook. Together, these twenty-one moves constitute a comprehensive inventory of the discursive strategies speakers use to manage trust.

The trust management function performed by the moves in our typology can be understood at different levels of granularity. At a fine-grained level, each move serves a distinct and specific function. For example, offering reassurances can foster trust by conveying empathy and concern or by addressing doubts about the speaker's intentions. This aligns with the 'benevolence' dimension of trustworthiness (Mayer et al. 1995). However, it is also possible – and indeed, given their large number, useful – to group the moves into broader categories that describe more general functions shared among them. Based on our analysis and theoretical insights from trust theory, we propose dividing the twenty-one moves in our taxonomy into five functional macro-categories: 'bond', 'build', 'confide', 'probe', and 'repair'. We argue that these macro-categories capture the five core discursive processes on which trust management relies.

Table 6 A typology of trust management moves.

Move	Corpus example
Apologize	BB: Hey. I'm sorry about that gen. I feel - you know - like an idiot. But I don't know what the guy was doing.
Boast	BW: Is there any shit goin' down MU: No, we're just makin' money hand over fist. BW: Shut up. MU: We are, Dude. BW: What? MU: We're going to be over 2 G's to 200 G's.
Commit	LR: Yeah, and in the future, I will, you know, yeah, D: I don't, you know, I'm not - LR: I'll - I'll be more communicative on that part.
Deny	MM: I mean, I continue to think, you know what? We did nothing wrong, you know? We - we took risk - J: Yeah. MM: Um, they fucked the market up. It's their - you know, it's their fault, it's not ours. We didn't do anything wrong. We weren't going to manipulate anything.
Express distrust/ doubt/skepticism	T: Yeh, [inaudible] we're very leery of those transactions, you do know that, right? JF: Yes, I do. T: OK, but if you're - if you're in a bind, yeah, I don't mind helping you.
Give warning	G: OK, I'm goin' to I - make a log of it. We're - we're creatin' a history of all this kind of activity, so - JB: I - I mean- G: Let's see if we're gon' put a stop to it.
Highlight advantages	SR: So all I'm saying is that to truly optimize your system this is a rare opportunity and we can offer you back money.

Table 6 (cont.)

Move	Corpus example
Inclusive framing	RS: Hey, I was just talking to the gen guys, I wanted to see if we could shut copper down. They weren't sure if ah, if there were any issues, or, ah [coughs]. Excuse me. Is that something that's ah, that's available to us to do, or?
Justify	MI: Are you guys selling anything at Mead? I got – I'm looking for ten megawatts. J: Mike, if I had it, ah, I would love to sell it to you, but right now I am tapped out completely MI: Really?
Keep options open	BW: And, ah, and maybe, you know, maybe, I don't know, maybe sell your generation out of market. Do whatever you feel you need to do there. That's – that's up to you.
Offer reassurance	M: Yeah, um, Chris, we – we're gonna turn the burner on and j – and just kinda get us up to schedule until we further understand what – what is goin' on here. CF: OK. I'm pretty confident that you're not gonna be incurring penalties until Tuesday.
Praise	PC: That is beautiful. You've done a great job negotiating.
Share emotions	JL: Yeah. [inaudible] fuck, this isn't a joke. I'm a little – nobody else seems to be concerned anymore about it, except for me.
Share privileged information	PC: Yeah. So, ah, what we need to do is to help in the cause of ah, downfall of California – n – [chuckles] and I – it's not [inaudible], it's economic decision-wise, you guys need to pull your megawatts out of California on a daily basis –

Trust, Discourse, and Corporate Corruption

Table 6 (cont.)

Move	Corpus example
	S: Yeah.
	PC: –whatever you have, and sell it in the bi-lateral market.
Shift the blame	MM: I mean, I continue to think, you know what? We did nothing wrong, you know? We – we took risk –
	J: Yeah.
	MM: Um, they fucked the market up. It's their – you know, it's their fault, it's not ours. We didn't do anything wrong. We weren't going to manipulate anything.
Show agreement	D: People just can't, are not, unless gas costs come down, you know, he's gotta shut down generation.
	LR: You're absolutely correct and that's exactly what's happening.
Show concern for the interlocutor	D: Yeah, I – we're – we're really exposed with the governor involved in this, and -
	SR: How do you feel about it?
	D: It's y – ah, we really need to try and avoid that kind of [inaudible] –
Show transparency	JF: She's very upset with us and has said that this is a phantom schedule and she's going to report us for non-compliance and blah, blah, blah. So, ah, what I'm trying to do is explain to you exactly what kind of deal this is.
	J: Mm hm.
Show trust	MM: Ah, you work it however you see fit, man, that's why you get paid the big bucks.
Show understanding/ empathize	D: Um, I guess the first – I – I really – I – I – I just really want to apologize for all this – this aggravation and – and everything. It – it's just been, ah, you know. I'm sure very frustrating for you and it's been extremely frustrating for me.

Table 6 (cont.)

Move	Corpus example
Signal confidentiality	JF: Yeah, and I - she's re - really, really upset with us and you see, the way this works out is we're an SC for somebody and - J: Right. JF: - this - this m- you know in between me and you - J: Mm hm. JF: Unofficially, I guess. J: Right.

The five macro-categories of trust management and their corresponding moves are shown in Table 7. 'Bond' encompasses moves used to foster emotional connection and a sense of alignment between participants. These moves mainly act to convey and consolidate perceptions of benevolence – the feeling that the speaker genuinely cares for the hearer beyond selfish motives (Mayer et al. 1995). We argue that 'bond' is the primary discursive mechanism through which 'affect-based trust' develops (McAllister 1995). The 'build' category includes moves geared towards demonstrating the speaker's ability and intention to fulfill tasks important to the hearer. This directly relates to 'cognition-based trust' (McAllister 1995), providing rational arguments for why the hearer should trust the speaker. The third communicative function, 'confide', involves sharing sensitive and potentially harmful information. By confiding, the speaker demonstrates trust by displaying vulnerability, which, in turn, can help strengthen the relationship. Trust, however, is not always a given. Speakers often use language to challenge or test the trustworthiness of their interlocutor, a function we term 'probe'. Finally, when trust is damaged or at risk, speakers employ moves to repair it, including accommodating strategies (e.g., 'apologize') and defensive strategies (e.g., 'shift the blame'). These five macro categories add theoretical depth to our taxonomy, revealing potentially universal discursive processes of trust management and offering a principled way to aggregate and interpret our results.

It is important to emphasize that context plays a vital role in the analysis of discursive trust management, as indeed in any form of discourse analysis. While some moves in our typology, such as 'show trust' or 'signal confidentiality', are inherently associated with trust and therefore consistently perform a trust

Table 7 Core trust management functions and corresponding moves.

Communicative function	Move
Bond	Inclusive framing
	Offer reassurance
	Praise
	Share emotions
	Show agreement
	Show concern for interlocutor
	Show understanding/empathize
	Show trust
Build	Boast
	Commit
	Highlight advantages
	Keep options open
Confide	Signal confidentiality
	Share privileged information
Probe	Express distrust/doubt/skepticism
	Give warning
Repair	Apologize
	Deny
	Justify
	Shift the blame
	Show transparency

management function, others are more flexible and may serve different pragmatic purposes depending on the context. For instance, 'show agreement' only functions as a trust management device when it is used to express alignment with and validate the other person's feelings or perspective, as shown in Extract 3 (lines 5, 6). More perfunctory "factual" instances of agreement that do not serve this bonding function, such as Extract 4 (line 5), should be excluded from the analysis.

Extract 3. Source document: SNO-415, 04/08/2000.

```
1   C:   Yeah, prices of homes have increased four hundred percent and
2        you - your power bills haven't increased in twenty years.
3   MM:  [chuckling]
4   C:   [chuckling] Get a fuckin' clue.
5   MM:  Yeah. Leave us alone. Let us a make a little bit of money.
6   C:   Yeah, exactly.
```

Extract 4. Source document: SNO-577, 02/07/2000.

```
1    MU:   Hey. How are you, sir?
2    J:    Hey, pretty good. Um, for hour ending 15?
3    MU:   Yeah.
4    J:    You guys have an export schedule at PV, PX, EPMI10 50?
5    MU:   Correct.
```

Similarly, not all apologies contribute to trust repair; routine or procedural apologies, such as those offered for mishearing or misunderstanding, carry no clear implications for trust and should not be coded as trust relevant (see codebook for examples). In our analysis, we closely considered the context in which each move appeared. We only coded instances of the moves from our framework that, based on our best understanding of the communicative situation and the interaction, appeared to serve a trust management function, as defined in the codebook.

Another important aspect to consider in discursive trust management analysis is that some utterances may simultaneously perform more than one move. For example, in Extract 5, Enron's SC shifts the blame for limitations of the 'Ricochet' trading strategy onto others while also expressing strong negative emotions about the situation (lines 4, 6–8). Accordingly, these stretches of talk should be coded as performing both the 'shift the blame' and 'share emotions' moves.

Extract 5. Source document: SNO-365, 03/08/2000.

```
1    G:    [inaudible] I know, but like I said before, we were definitely,
2          ah - we got - we milked it longer than anybody else for sure.
3    SC:   [laughs] Yeah! That's so fuckin' stupid, though, it drives me
4          fuckin' insane - I - god! People are so fuckin' stupid.
5    G:    I know.
6    SC:   So [inaudible] is a whole bunch of transactions that won't
7          occur now because people can't net schedule and it won't raise
8          the revenue of the fuckin' transmission people at all.
```

To account for instances where a stretch of discourse performs multiple trust management functions, we allowed for double coding in our analysis. However, this was applied sparingly and only when clearly justified by the contextual evidence.

Lastly, some of the moves in our framework may, in certain contexts, be seen to perform multiple trust management macro-functions. For example, boasting can sometimes serve as a form of bonding, particularly when both speakers participate in it and jointly celebrate shared achievements. In light of this, it is important to emphasize that the categorization presented in Table 7 reflects what we identified, based on our analysis, as the primary trust management function of each move. However, this classification should not be applied rigidly; contextual sensitivity is essential for an accurate and nuanced analysis. Discursive trust management analysis is, above all, a qualitative and interpretive process that must remain grounded in context. While we do incorporate quantitative data from the corpus to highlight patterns and support our observations, it is vital that analysts remain attuned to the specific contexts in which trust management moves occur and to the 'local' functions they serve.

5.2 Quantitative Distribution of Trust Management Moves

Figure 7 shows the quantitative distribution of the five core trust management functions within the ETTC. This broad overview is complemented by a more detailed set of quantitative results that compare the normalized frequency of each individual move in the speech of Enron versus other speakers (Figure 8). These results, derived from the number of words coded for each category, provide a valuable "panoramic" perspective on Enron's discursive trust work and a useful lens to guide the qualitative analysis.

Our analysis reveals that a larger share of Enron's discourse was dedicated to trust management compared to other speakers, with 262.53 annotated words per thousand versus 224.99. This finding suggests a heightened need for trust

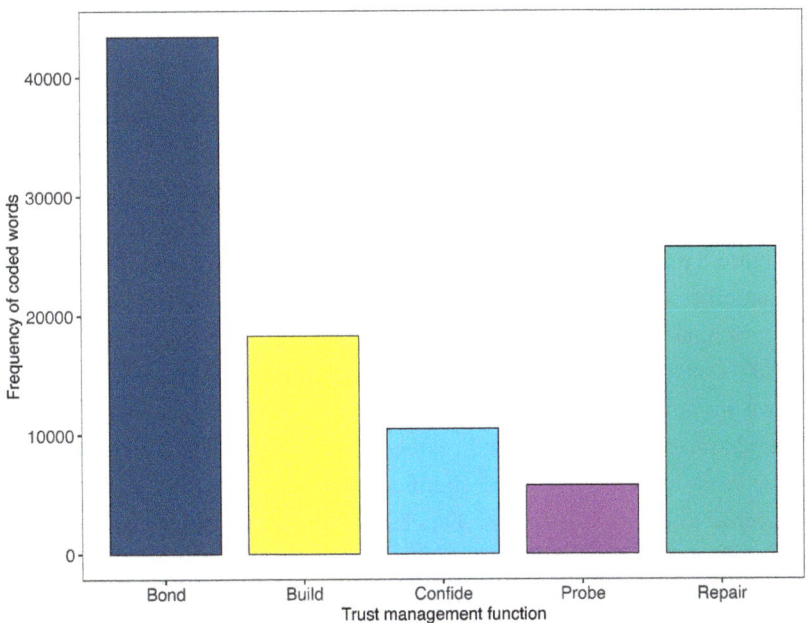

Figure 7 Distribution of macro trust management functions in the ETTC.

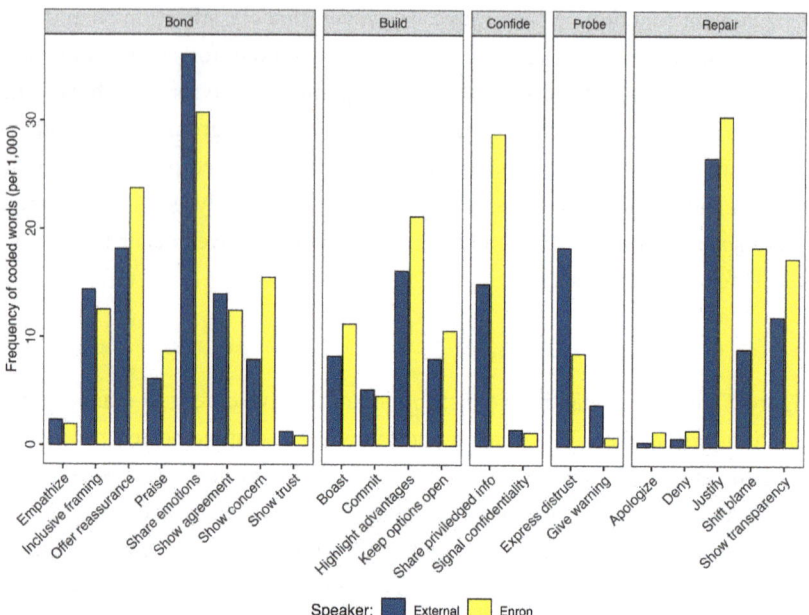

Figure 8 Distribution of trust management moves in the ETTC.

management in Enron's communication, which was likely driven by a combination of factors. The high-stakes and contentious nature of its business dealings during the California energy crisis, coupled with intensified scrutiny of its actions, placed Enron's trustworthiness under severe pressure. This pressure, in turn, increased the need for reactive discursive trust management. But the elevated frequency of trust-related discourse could also indicate a deliberate and proactive attempt to shape perceptions, ensuring clients, regulators, and other stakeholders remained confident in Enron's intentions despite their underlying fraudulent activities.

Figure 8 provides details about the specific moves used by Enron traders versus other speakers, offering additional insights into the communicative motives underpinning their linguistic behavior. The results show that 'bond' was the dominant trust management function in the ETTC, as shown by both its textual coverage and by the diverse range of moves it encompasses. Within the 'bond' category, the moves 'show concern' and 'offer reassurance' were used significantly more often by Enron traders compared to external speakers. This higher frequency suggests that Enron traders devoted considerable discursive effort to building affective ties with their interlocutors and alleviating potential doubts or anxieties about their intentions or actions. The pattern for 'share emotions' moves supports this interpretation, as external speakers were observed to use this move more often, suggesting that Enron traders sought to project the persona of a "friendly and supportive listener". Another 'bond' move that stood out in Enron's discourse was 'praise'. As discussed further in Section 5.4, Enron traders used this move mainly in internal calls to compliment each other on successful business decisions, alongside 'boast' to showcase their own achievements.

Within the 'build' category, all moves except 'commit' were used more frequently by Enron traders compared to external speakers. As discussed in greater detail below, these moves were used persuasively to project competence and convince clients to support Enron's proposed deals and market operations. Unsurprisingly, within the 'confide' category, Enron speakers shared privileged information significantly more often than external speakers. In our codebook, privileged information is defined as "private, morally or legally ambiguous, and potentially damaging information". For Enron, this primarily involved sharing details about their market gaming strategies. However, while the 'share privileged information' move was far less common in the speech of external speakers, it remains noticeably present. This suggests active cooperation and mutual information-sharing between Enron and selected external partners in advancing Enron's strategies, regardless of whether those partners were fully aware of the legality or implications of those strategies. Expressions of distrust and warnings were predominantly voiced by external speakers, which reflects the fact that the California crisis and the traders' activities had raised significant doubts about Enron's trustworthiness. In response, Enron traders engaged in trust repair discourse more frequently than other speakers, adopting primarily defensive moves such as 'justify' and 'shift the blame'. The more conciliatory 'show transparency' move was also commonly used. By contrast, apologies and outright denials were rare.

5.3 Qualitative Analysis of Trust Management Moves in Context

These quantitative results can help us identify broad patterns in the corpus and suggest potential overarching strategies employed by Enron traders. However, to gain a deeper and more nuanced understanding of their discursive behavior, we need to examine how the trust management moves were used in specific contexts. One of the key advantages of our methodology is that the manual coding process involves carefully reading and analyzing the texts in our corpus, yielding a very detailed, context-sensitive picture of how and why the moves were deployed. In this section, we highlight key insights from this qualitative analysis to offer a more precise understanding of the discursive and strategic functions of some of the most salient moves in the ETTC.

As seen above, the move 'share emotions' was pervasive in the corpus. Our qualitative analysis reveals that Enron traders often used this move in internal conversations as well as with external clients to complain about the California government's regulatory interventions designed to bring the energy crisis under control. In Extract 6, for example, Enron's MM responds to client Tom's concerns about recent developments in the crisis by expressing emotionally charged views against the recently introduced energy price caps and blaming the State of California for the energy shortages. MM frames the new measures as irrational interference with market forces, a narrative that Enron traders deployed repeatedly in the corpus to justify their actions. Extract 6 also features several instances of the 'show agreement' move, where agreement takes on a distinctly emotional tone. Both speakers engage in reciprocal displays of support for the other's affective stance – referred to as 'affiliation' (e.g., Couper-Kuhlen 2012; Stivers 2008) – through repeats (lines 12, 23), congruent negative assessments (lines 6, 9, 26), and acknowledgment tokens (line 21). Taken together, these discursive strategies allowed Enron traders to cultivate trust by fostering emotional bonds both internally and with clients, aligning themselves against a common adversary (i.e., the State of California), and projecting sincerity and genuine conviction in their modus operandi in a broad effort to legitimize their risky and potentially unlawful business practices.

Extract 6. Source document: SNO-230, 03/08/2000.

```
1    T:   Serious shit goin' on out in the West, man.
2    MM:  Why? What's goin' on? Record -
3    T:   Clinton steppin' in and stuff -
4    MM:  What's that?
5    T:   You see's Clinton steps in?
6    MM:  Oh, yeah, you see this shit? - Fuckin' nutty, huh?
7    T:   And he frickin' telling Bonneville they have to max deliver
8         whatever they can deliver.
9    MM:  Yeah, that's a bunch of bullshit. You know what - you know what
10        really pisses me off?
11   T:   The price caps?
12   MM:  The price caps! You know what -?
13   T:   Fucking bullshit. It would take care of all the weak. Get 'em
14        out.
15   MM:  Y - you know what they're doin'? They're selling the fuckin'
16        fish in Oregon to our State of California for a fuckin' 250
```

```
17        dollars.
18   T:   They w - oh, yeah! Yeah.
19   MM:  You know why, because - because they're shutting off the
20        spill -
21   T:   Yeah.
22   MM:  They're killing fuckin' thousands of fish.
23   T:   They're killing fish, right? Yeah.
24   MM:  Um, and there would be ample supply available at the right
25        fuckin' price.
26   T:   Oh, sure there would.
```

The 'inclusive framing' move served a similar solidarity and consensus-building function, fostering a sense of unity of purpose both internally among Enron traders and externally with clients and business partners. For example, in Extract 7, this move is deployed to highlight the mutual benefits of Enron managing its client's generation requirements, promoting trust in both Enron's market acumen and genuine care towards the client (lines 11, 16–21).

Extract 7. Source document: SNO-434, 15/09/2000.

```
1    PC:  Um, well. August was a good month for both Enron and, ah,
2         [company name].
3    L:   Yeah!
4    PC:  Um, you should be getting an invoice today to, ah -
5    L:   We gonna owe you another 300,000 dollars this month?
6    PC:  You gonna owe us, ah, North the 300,000 dollars, but it's gonna
7         be -
8    L:   No, I mean, next - for this next month - for September.
9    PC:  For September?
10   L:   Yeah, the more I owe you, the less it costs me, you know.
11   PC:  Well, that's where we're aligned. The incentives are aligned.
12        And ah-
13   L:   That's what I say.
14   PC:  I'm sorry?
15   L:   That's what I say.
16   PC:  Yeah - that's why - that's why this is beautiful. You - we
17        don't win unless you guys win, and if neither of us wins,
18        then, ah, we've - you know what I mean, it's all al - the
19        incentives are aligned, so that's - that's what, ah, the
20        whole purpose of this, all, remarketing value was. So, it's
21        working to, ah, form.
22   L:   Right. So I'll-I'm willing to pay you another three hundred
23        thousand next month.
```

As shown in Extract 8, 'inclusive framing' (lines 9–10, "what *we* can do with Copper") was also used in conversations between Enron and power plant operators to coordinate operational actions. By framing actions as a collaborative effort – taking the "Copper" power generator offline in this case – Enron traders actively promoted a sense of alignment of intents, shared responsibility, and joint strategic decision-making. In turn, it provided Enron's traders with operational discretion over client infrastructure, which could be used to suppress energy supply, deploy tactics, and artificially inflate prices.

Extract 8. Source document: SNO-173, 10/09/2000.

```
1   P:    [company name].
2   BW:   Hey, this is Bill again. Yeah, uh, you were right, double ID
3         was dragging their feet. They're gonna go down to a 130.
4   P:    130.
5   BW:   Or - excuse me, 120. My goodness.
6   P:    120?
7   BW:   Yeah 120 for 23.
8   P:    Shit, that's a big cut, man. OK, what else?
9   BW:   Uh, that's it. I'd like to watch, uh, what we can do with
10        Copper?
11  P:    Yeah, maybe we can take it off.
12  BW:   Yeah, I'd like to start rollin' it.
13  P:    Yeah, we can start takin' it off right now, eh? Well, 109,
14        still man. [inaudible] are kinda low.
```

As noted earlier, several high-frequency 'bond' moves indicate that Enron traders, as part of their trust management strategy, aimed to project a supportive and engaged persona in their interactions with outsiders. This is clearly illustrated in Extract 9, where Enron's PC employs the 'offer reassurance' move (lines 10–11, 15–17) to alleviate client concerns about the impact of the newly imposed price caps amidst the escalating California energy crisis. As part of this reassurance, he provides a confident prediction about future price trends, supported by sensory evidentiality (line 15, "we've seen") for enhanced credibility. Through this approach, PC positions himself as both a caring and attentive business partner while also signaling competence. In terms of Mayer et al.'s (1995) model, this segment of discourse is designed to project both benevolence and ability.

Extract 9. Source document: SNO-452, 15/12/2000.

```
1   E:    Ho - how - ho - how far - ah, what were the - were the numbers
2         that I threw out, ah, ah, fairly accurate?
3   PC:   What, for the 150 dollar, 250 dollar cap?
4   B:    No, the 80 - 80 to 100 dollar off peak.
5   PC:   Uh, for what period, the Q1 period?
6   B:    Yeah.
7   PC:   Ah, yeah, that's probably right in the ball park, it might be a
8         little bit higher. Ah, right now the FERC came out with the
9         ruling on California, imposing 150 dollar price caps, ah, in
10        the state of California, but that doesn't - that's not gonna
```

```
11           affect you guys as much, ah - in general, I mean, it's - it's
12           gonna probably depress the prices a little bit throughout the
13           west.
14    E:     Yup.
15    PC:    Ah, but it - it still, I mean, we've seen prices, for instance
16           in the northwest, trade above whatever price cap imposition
17           that, ah, California has put out there.
```

The 'bond' moves 'show concern' and 'show understanding-empathize' were similarly deployed to project "genuine" care towards clients, particularly when delivering bad news. This language helped Enron traders foster an image of honest (integrity) and caring (benevolence) business consultants. In Extract 10, for example, Enron's CF shows concern towards a client by warning them about the risk of rolling blackouts in California following recent emergency measures announced by the ISO (lines 14–15, 17–18). He then emphatically communicates sympathy to the client (lines 27–28, 33, 38). Ironically, Enron's own actions significantly contributed to those very blackouts. This stark contrast exposes the performative nature of these verbal displays of trustworthiness, raising doubts about the trader's sincerity.

Extract 10. Source document: SNO-301, 05/12/2000.

```
1     CF:    Now if they - if they allow prices to go up. See and what -
2            they have this thing called out-of-market where they can just
3            go out and buy it uh, in an emergency situation. So they just
4            talk to the utilities and if they're - you know - able through
5            a back door to cut a deal so that the lights don't go out. But
6            it's possible that the lights could go out. And in fact
7            somebody just hollered a few minutes ago that uh - there's a
8            press release that the ISO has issued. That's the people who
9            run the grid.
10    T:     Mm hm.
11    CF:    Saying that there's a significant chance of rolling brown outs
12           this winter in California.
13    T:     Hmm.
14    CF:    So the chances - the point of that is you're going to get
15           interrupted.
16    [...]
17    CF:    Yeah. You're gonna get interrupted whatever the maximum is -
18           count on it.
19    T:     Alright.
20    CF:    Okay?
21    T:     Fuck!
22    CF:    It's not a pret - pretty sight.
23    T:     Fuc - I gotta find me a real - a job with not so many frickin'
24           God Damn bullets with my name on it.
25    CF:    [laughing]
26    T:     Holy Shit.
```

```
27   CF:   I feel your pain man. You had a tough go of it in the last
28         year.
29   T:    Well. I think - just think if [inaudible] was here. He'd have a
30         - he fucking would have a meltdown already.
31   CF:   [laughing]
32   T:    He would - he fucking ought to have had a breakdown.
33   CF:   I hear 'ya. It's been.
34   T:    He couldn't handle the fucking - just the normal operation
35         bullshit. [chuckling]
36   CF:   Yeah.
37   T:    Oh accept these fucking leader's curve ball.
38   CF:   It's tough. You got a lot going on there.
```

As noted earlier, 'repair' was the second most frequent trust management function in the ETTC, which highlights the ongoing pressure Enron faced to maintain trust during the California energy crisis. Trust repair discourse was often directed at agents of the California ISO, the State's electricity grid operator, who on several occasions questioned Enron's scheduling activities. In Extract 11, for instance, ISO agent George expresses distrust toward Enron's JB after JB reports that Enron can no longer fulfill an electricity schedule, allegedly due to unforeseen circumstances. George repeatedly challenges this explanation, accusing JB of "playing games" by knowingly bidding on a schedule without securing the actual energy to fulfill it. In response, JB employs different defensive 'repair' moves, specifically 'deny' (lines 13, 15, 21), 'justify' (lines 10, 11), and 'shift the blame' (lines 15–17), to counter the ISO agent's accusations and restore trust.

Extract 11. Source document: SNO-815, undated.

```
1    JB:   Hey, George?
2    G:    Yeah.
3    JB:   Um, for 23 hundred pe - ah, the schedule was cut - generator
4          was cut, so we cannot show up with those megawatts. Both
5          [company name] and [company name] cut'em.
6    G:    So you - what are you sayin' then? Wha-
7    JB:   I'm sayin' I-I will not be showing up with those megawatts. The
8          schedule's gonna go to zero for 23--
9    G:    But you've already been awarded the bid. [beep]
10   JB:   We've been tryin' to fill it. I mean, we've been on the phone
11         for a half hour straight
12   G:    So you were actually biddin' a schedule that you can't -
13   JB:   No we - we had -
14   G:    - you can't fulfill and, ah, is what you're tellin' me, huh?
15   JB:   We had it filled - we had it filled- we bought-I mean, we were
16         gettin' it from [company name] and [company name] and then
17         bottom of the hour, I mean, they cut
18   G:    N - actually what you're doin' is you're playing games. You're
```

```
19         biddin' in the schedule in - in hopes of gettin' the energy and
20         when you don't really have it to start with.
21   JB:   That - no, we had the energy. We had the energy- I mean -
```

Trust repair moves were not only found in conversations with market operators. On several occasions, Enron traders also needed to repair trust with their own clients and business partners. A remarkable example of this is the conversation below between Enron's SR and Ron, an employee from a client firm. This conversation is cited in multiple instances in the court documents, including an expert witness testifying to Enron's counterparties' concerns regarding the manipulation of market prices through the EnronOnline (EOL), the company's proprietary web-based trading platform. The tape is also used to argue that Enron used EOL to manipulate prices, exercise market power, and deceive customers.

In Extract 12, Ron brings up a problem he has experienced with EOL when the price for the energy he wanted mysteriously increased after attempting to initiate the transaction. Ron perceives the unexpected price increase as an anomaly. He recounts his experience over several turns, expressing surprise and unease (lines 2–4, 17–20, 27–28), openly voicing suspicion towards EOL agents (32–35), and seeking clarification from SR.

Extract 12. Source document: SNO-508, 08/01/2001.

```
1    SR:   So, you were able to get coverage from -
2    R:    It worked - we - it - it - it - but I tell you, ah, you left
3          kind of a - a bad taste in our mouth the way it came down, and
4          it might have been just a coincidence, but -
5    SR:   What happened?
6    R:    Well, I got on Enrononline.
7          [...]
8    R:    And, um, so I said, yeah, hey, go ahead and get it. So I get
9          on Enrononline and look at the prices and there it is, the
10         price was 140. I'm goin' OK, I want to hit that, and, um, I -
11         I really needed 50, is what I wanted to pick up, but then I
12         go, I'll get the 25 first. Well, I get this message - you
13         know, I get this error m - not an error message, but prompt
14         that said, ah, you know, it's denied - you know, transaction
15         denied, um, you - you need to call,
16         [...]
17   R:    Yeah. Anyway, um, y - th - what was - what was eerie was like
18         they knew who I was, what I was lookin' at, and I mean, pretty
19         well just - I guess they, you know, you guys - or Enrononline
20         can tell on the other side what - what we're lookin' at.
21         [...]
22   R:    So then what happ - It - I explained the t - situation, and -
23         and what I wanted to do. He, you know, he said, well, I'll
```

```
24           have to call Houston and - and find out why, you know, this
25           didn't take 'cause it should have and all this and - and, you
26           know, do you still want to do this and I went, yeah, and - and
27           as I'm lookin' at the screen, all of a sudden the price goes
28           from 140 to 155. And I'm thinkin' -
29   SR:     Well, what I would have said -
30   R:      And I'm thinkin', now wait a minute, you know - ?
31           [...]
32           I probably could buy the other one for 155, so they just made
33           it look like as soon as I wanted to buy it, they went, Oh,
34           this - you know, there's some interest here, let's move the
35           price up. It just looked kind of- [inaudible]
```

Extract 12 effectively illustrates the interplay between interpersonal and situational trust (see Section 2.1). Ron's experience represents a breach of situational trust, as the transaction deviated from the expected and normal sequence of events. This disruption, in turn, raises doubts about Enron's integrity and benevolence, suggesting that Enron traders may have been covertly monitoring the client's actions and manipulating prices for their own benefit. Ron explicitly raises the issue of trust, compelling SR to undertake a sustained discursive effort to address his concerns and work toward restoring trust, as shown in Extract 13.

Extract 13. Source document: SNO-508, 08/01/2001.

```
1    SR:     No, no, do you see, what it could be is a lot of times there's
2            not a lot of supply out there and these guys can't do a 50
3            megawatt transaction and -
4    R:      Uh huh.
5    SR:     - even if you wanted to do 50 megawatts all at once on EOL, it
6            only lets you do it in 25 increments.
7    R:      Yeah?
8    SR:     So it might say, look, you gotta do the first 25 and then give
9            the trader the chance to reset the price and then they could
10           have pulled the product. So -
11   R:      OK
12   SR:     - I don't think that - obviously if he had it to sell, he
13           would have just said, well, my next 25, I would have sol - I -
14           I'll sell to you at whatever price.
15   R:      Yeah.
16   SR:     If he says, I'm not selling it, it means he just doesn't have
17           it and doesn't want to get short.
18   R:      OK
19   SR:     Which - given how s - how little the liquidity is, that would
20           be my - I mean, I guess Paul probably didn't realize what you
21           were thinking, or he sh - would have explained that to you.
22   R:      Yeah.
23   SR:     You know, if - if, ah - if you're on the phone with us trying
```

24		to work out an EOL issue that you were trying to do something
25		at 140 and also the price jumps to 155 and they try to stick
26		you with the 155, I think you've totally a legitimate argument
27		to say, Look, I tried to do something at 140, the price
28		changed -
29	R:	Yeah.
30	SR:	- while we were trying to do this, please keep me whole on the
31		initial number. But, if they only showed a 25 megawatt offer.
32	R:	[inaudible] it did say, just 25.
33	SR:	Yeah. I don't think - I - I honestly don't think they were
34		trying to -
35	R:	OK.
36	SR:	I mean he didn't - he didn't sell to you the second 25 at a
37		higher price either, right?
38	R:	No, I didn't buy the second piece.
39	SR:	Right so he didn't benefit - I mean -
40	R:	No -
41	SR:	By ha - by knowing you were trying to buy 50, he didn't
42		benefit -
43	R:	No.
44	SR:	- on the second piece.
45	R:	No.
46	SR:	I really just think he didn't have it to sell.
47	R:	OK.
48	SR:	Well, I - I apologize I wasn't here, 'cause it's better to
49		resolve it right away, make sure you're comfortable with it.
50	R:	Yeah, it just - you know, but is it coincidence that the
51		trader, you know, pulled the price up? It just is interes -
52	SR:	And - and where was it, was it Palo, or -
53	R:	It was, ah, SP.
54	SR:	SP.
55	R:	Yeah.
56	SR:	So, it was probably Bob [surname], and, ah, he just might not
57		have had anything to sell.
58	R:	Yeah, it was Bob. That was the guy.
59	SR:	Yeah.
60	R:	That - that name sounds familiar. That was the trader.
61	SR:	Well I - I'm back, so in the future - I'd really like to know
62		what happened to your EOL - why you couldn't transact there,
63		'cause that's [inaudible] -
64	R:	Ah, well, Paul called back and said it was all squared away.
65	SR:	All right.

To restore situational trust, SR initiates a prolonged 'justify' move, rationalizing and reframing the situation to present it as logical and reinstating a sense of normalcy to the events. Through this detailed explanation, he positions himself as an "expert guide", reinforcing his competence and authority. He attributes the sudden price shift to the 25-megawatt cap on the amount of energy EOL traders can sell in a single transaction (lines 5–6), a limitation Ron was apparently unaware of. SR explains that this cap could cause price fluctuations after the initial transaction, as prices are reset and recalculated based on the available supply following each trade (lines 8–10). In this way, the unexpected price increase is reframed as a typical outcome of EOL trading practices and operational constraints, rather than a deliberate effort to exploit the client. Throughout Extract 13, SR repeatedly appeals to Ron's 'logos', aiming to convince him of the credibility of his account. For instance, in line 12, he uses the epistemic adverb 'obviously' to present the argument that the EOL trader lacked the energy Ron sought at the initial price as commonsensical. Furthermore, in lines 36–44, he carefully guides Ron to the logical conclusion that there was no deceit because the EOL trader did not personally benefit from accepting the higher offer. Ron's positive response, "OK" (line 47), indicates he accepts this explanation.

SR employs a range of trust-management moves alongside 'justify', with a focus on repairing perceptions of Enron's benevolence. In lines 20–21, 33–34, and 46, he uses the 'offer reassurance' move to alleviate any doubts that the EOL trader sought to exploit Ron. Furthermore, he uses a combination of the 'apology' (lines 48–49), 'show concern for interlocutor' (lines 49), and 'commit' (lines 61–63) moves to convey his personal remorse for the situation, express his commitment to avoiding similar incidents in the future, and demonstrate his personal investment in the relationship.

The third most common trust management function in the ECCT was 'build', with the most frequent move within this category being 'highlight advantages'. Enron traders used this move to foster trust in their competent leadership and persuade clients to follow their advice, particularly regarding strategic market plays. This is exemplified in Extract 14, where SR emphasizes the success of the existing partnership with client Dick (lines 3–4) and repeatedly frames his new proposal as an "opportunity" (lines 6, 12). Enron traders also frequently used the 'keep options open' move in communications and negotiations with clients to demonstrate flexibility and address concerns about potential risks or opportunistic behavior. Such discursive work would have been especially important at the height of the California energy crisis when uncertainty and public scrutiny were high. This is evident in Extract 14, where Dick voices concerns about SR's proposal to establish a contract for transferring electricity out of California's grid (lines 21–22, 24–25). By framing the proposal in tentative, exploratory terms, SR seeks to maintain Dick's trust while navigating the politically sensitive issue of exporting electricity during the California energy crisis. This strategic flexibility appears to be designed to reassure the client that their partnership prioritizes mutual benefit, even as Enron explores potentially lucrative but controversial opportunities.

Extract 14. Source document: SNO-380, 05/12/2000.

```
 1 SR: OK, we'll there - there's a couple things I wanted to ask you
 2      about, um, with respect to transmission and perhaps the answer
 3      is we just keep doing what we're doing now which seems to be
 4      working pretty well, but to the extent we could do something,
 5      ah, in the term - balance of the month and term, there might
 6      be some other opportunities. There is two things that we're
 7      looking at trying to do with people: The first is there is
 8      opportunity to move energy on a term basis, like balance of
 9      the month or next month - January on peak hours from SP or NP-
10      15 up to COB, that what we're doing right now is unknown
11      quantities of transmission, so obviously we can't lock in any
12      kind of spread, but there's opportunity for us to say to you,
13      hey, if we know that we have on-peak hours, we can give you
14      this much money per megawatt hour for, you know, this term for
15      this many megawatt hours. The problem is, I don't know if
16      that's possible, given - I mean is your feel that even at 25
17      megawatt level, there'd be an ability to carve out something,
18      consistently?
19 D:   Would that be going up to COB on our transmission?
20 SR:  Yeah, COB South to North.
21 D:   Yeah the - yeah, that got a real political dilemma right now
22      with [inaudible] -
23 SR:  Ah, about taking power outside the grid.
24 D:   Yeah, I - we're - we're really exposed with the governor
25      involved in this, and -
```

The quantitative analysis revealed a prominent role for 'confide' moves, particularly 'share privileged information', within the ETTC. This finding suggests that a substantial portion of the conversations involved explicit discussions of potentially illicit market manipulation practices, plans, and decisions. For example, in Extract 15, taken from an internal call, Enron traders JF and BW are openly talking about and celebrating the success of their 'Death Star' trading strategy (see Section 3.2), which involved faking energy transmission schedules in a loop going the opposite way of a jammed path to get paid for "fixing" the congestion. By sharing privileged information and coordinating their actions, Enron traders and colluding actors successfully manipulated the market, simultaneously strengthening the mutual trust that was essential for continued collaboration and the achievement of their objectives.

Extract 15. Source document: SNO-324, 04/08/2000.

```
1   JF:  How did we make it? Was it con - 'con-gestion' [French accent]?
2   BW:  A lot of it was 'cong'. We made 35 grand on 'cong' in one hour.
3   JF:  Oh, my gosh.
4   BW:  'Cong' actually looks like it's one - half of it's 'cong' - 167
5        is 'cong'.
6   JF:  Oh, my gosh.
7   BW:  Death Star pulled in a solid, like, 24 and then load shifts
8        picked up 140 grand.
9   JF:  Wow. That's crazy, man. I hope you guys - oh, no man - this c -
10       this can't go on.
11  BW:  And that - they're just giving away money.
```

The substantial use of 'share privileged information' in recorded telephone conversations suggests that Enron's traders and their associates either underestimated the risk of getting caught or the illicit implications of their actions. Textual evidence supports the latter explanation, as traders frequently offered justifications for their decisions, framing them as normal and unproblematic. In Extract 16, for example, TB defends Enron West Power's strategy to a senior Public Affairs executive from Enron's main corporate headquarters in Houston. He employs a utilitarian justification, seeking to reframe the division's questionable behavior as permissible given the ambiguities within existing regulations (lines 19–22). In Extract 17, MM rationalizes Enron's exporting of power – a move that intensified California's shortages and price volatility – as a logical response to market conditions. He attributes the dysfunction to California's price cap, arguing that it suppressed in-state prices below levels available in neighboring markets, thereby encouraging exports. MM frames Enron's actions not as opportunistic manipulation, but as merely following "price signals" (lines 11–13, 25–26), absolving Enron of responsibility while participating in and benefiting from the very crisis its traders had helped develop.

Extract 16. Source document: SNO-220, 04/08/2000.

```
1   R:   Yeah, the other thing I just think, you know, and I - you know,
2        you guys, you know, I know, I s - I assume and trust are
3        playing completely within the rules, but you know, just be
4        cognizant of the fact that come - you know, I mean [FERC?] will
5        undertake, you know, an investigation, you know, this fall of
6        everything that's going on in California, so -
7   TB:  Right.
8   R:   - I mean I - you just have to - I think you just have to have
9        that in the back of your mind.
10  TB:  Yeah, w - we are - well, let me tell you a couple of things
11       that we've done.
12  R:   Yeah.
13  TB:  Um, there are um - a - and all of this stuff with - there's
```

Trust, Discourse, and Corporate Corruption

```
14        really two – two things that happened – two areas where we have
15        risk with the ISO in terms of not getting along with them or –
16        or things blowing up. Ah, one is our day-ahead scheduling
17        practices and then the other one is our real-time operations.
18   R:   Mm hm.
19   TB:  Um, we've been doing and have been doing for two years a lot of
20        activity in, you know, there's black, there's white and there's
21        gray. Um, we have been endeavoring into the gray area when
22        opportunities present themselves –
23   R:   Mm hm.
24   TB:  – to make money in real time. We have now moved out of the gray
25        area into the clearly what's legal area, a – and I'm – not even
26        legal, but what's, um, there's like the letter of the law, the
27        letter of the rules and the spirit of the rules.
```

Extract 17. Source document: SNO-414, 04/08/2000.

```
1    MM:  Yeah. Sorry California. I'm bringing all our power out of the
2         state. Today I moved out six – over six hundred megawatts.
3    B:   Did you really?
4    MM:  Mm hm. I bought it in California and moving it out to, uh,
5         Arizona and Nevada.
6    B:   Why are you doing that, though? I mean, it –
7    MM:  Because the prices are higher outside of the state.
8    B:   Oh – oh, because of the cap?
9    MM:  Exactly.
10   B:   Wow! That's unreal.
11   MM:  Yeah. So these guys are goin' "Oh, we're having a power
12        shortage [inaudible]. Well how do you indicate you're having a
13        shortage? Price signals.
14   B:   Right.
15   MM:  The other [inaudible] like outside of the state it's trading,
16        um, over that. So, I can make more money by moving my power out
17        of the state then by – then by leaving it in.
18   […]
19   MM:  Yeah. But it all depends, you know. On what Monika bids and
20        [yawning] unreal. Uh, so, yeah, it's pretty fucked up. But that
21        – you know, you just think about okay, if we're short or having
22        shortages of the power, what should you be doing? You should be
23        encouraging people to bring it into the state, right?
24   B:   Right.
25   MM:  Well, guess what. You're [sic] pricing mechanisms encourages
26        people to take it out of the state.
```

5.4 Distribution of Trust Management Moves Across Conversation Types

The ETTC is highly diverse in terms of both the interlocutors Enron traders engaged with and the content and goals of their conversations. The qualitative analysis suggests that Enron traders used different trust management strategies depending on their interlocutor and the content and overall purpose of the call. To further explore this important aspect and gain a more systematic understanding of how their discursive trust work was shaped by situational factors, we examined the distribution of the moves across sub-corpora created based on our three conversation-level codes: participants, nature of the call, and nature of the tie (see Section 4.4).

As far as call participants are concerned, the results show an overall higher relative density of trust management discourse in conversations between Enron traders and external speakers (287.14 per 1,000 words) compared to internal conversations (224.91 per 1,000 words). This pattern reflects the need for Enron traders to put more effort into building and maintaining trust with outsiders, whereas internal conversations may have relied on an already established level of trust among colleagues. The breakdown of specific trust management moves in Figure 9 adds nuance to this finding, highlighting notable differences in how Enron traders interacted with external versus internal speakers.

The quantitative results in Figure 9 confirm insights from the qualitative analysis, showing that Enron traders relied heavily on 'bond' moves such as 'offer reassurance' and 'show concern' when interacting with external speakers. As illustrated in Extracts 9 and 10, these moves were used to convey genuine care and interest toward clients, occasionally with manipulative intent, as seen in Extract 13. 'Inclusive framing' and 'show agreement' – both overrepresented in conversations with external speakers – were integral to the same overarching strategy of signaling benevolence and fostering a sense of collaboration. These moves aimed to make clients feel heard and included in Enron's success story.

The moves 'highlight advantages' and 'keep options open' were also key components of Enron's trust management with external speakers. They were often used in conversations about potential deals and business proposals to persuade clients, as shown in Extract 14 above. Within the 'repair' category, 'show transparency' was overwhelmingly more frequent in external calls compared to internal ones. This move commonly appeared in discussions with clients about a range of topics, including regulatory challenges, planning, business strategy, and profit-sharing agreements. Its overall purpose was to communicate integrity and preempt concerns that Enron traders might prioritize their own interests over those of their clients. For example, in Extract 18, Enron's LR addresses a client's question about how profit-sharing calculations were determined. By promising to "walk the client through the numbers" (lines 9–10), LR signals transparency, reinforcing

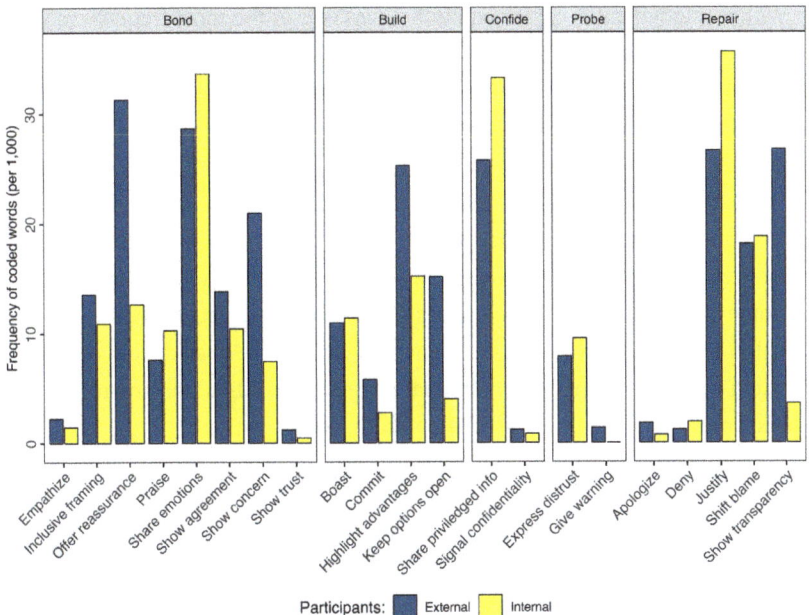

Figure 9 Distribution of trust management moves by 'participant' categories. Counts refer to moves used by Enron speakers only.

the message that everything is above board and Enron is not trying to take advantage of them.

Extract 18. Source document: SNO-372, 11/12/2000.

```
1   D:   Yeah. Hmm. Hey, one other issue aside, um, Fred called me, he's
2        at home, but he said he talked to Alan [surname] and he got a
3        contract from you guys?
4   LR:  Right.
5   D:   For 219 dollars?
6   LR:  Right.
7   D:   What's that about?
8        [...]
9   LR:  So, and I'll get you - I'll walk through the numbers with you
10       in the morning, but you're exactly right. Um, I said, just to
11       use round numbers here, say our generation costs was 100 bucks,
12       um, and all those other costs were 25, or whatever they were,
13       um, so, our - say our cost basis was 125, um, so we had a
14       profit of, um, and we sold it for 250 so we got a profit of a
15       hundred and a quarter. And so I did multiply that by s - by
16       seventy percent and, you know, that would be you guys share and
17       then the 30 percent is, um, is gonna be ours, so the way -
```

Within internal calls, 'share emotions' was one of the most frequent moves. This is likely at least in part due to the greater familiarity and intimacy among colleagues. However, as discussed above, emotion sharing also played a crucial role in building unity and legitimizing wrongdoing. By signaling emotional alignment, shared values, and a common enemy in those who "don't understand the market", Enron traders fostered a sense of camaraderie and legitimacy for their actions. Praising was also more frequent in Enron's internal calls. This move frequently co-occurred with 'boast', which was also marginally more common in internal calls. Employees celebrated their accomplishments and signaled approval to colleagues, as shown in Extract 19. In such conversations, boasting acted as a display of individual competence, while praising reinforced shared values and a relentless focus on profit maximization.

Extract 19. Source document: SNO-323, 04/08/2000.

```
1    MM:   We bought it - we bought it - we bought it from Seattle again.
2          We did that same deal with them that we did before.
3    JF:   Yeah?
4    MM:   Um, where, ah
5    JF:   The same deal, being, you know, you just - you just, ah, tell
6          them what you're doin' with it?
7    MM:   Yeah, I bought 450s and sold to the ISO at 490.
8    JF:   You're the man.
9    MM:   So -
10   JF:   Good.
11   MM:   Fifteen - it was like 75 megawatts, 15 through 18.
12   JF:   Yeah.
13   MM:   And ah, other than that we got - there's some cong today,
14         pretty good cong. We missed one hour because I - I thought
15         today that the cong wasn't going to be there like it was
16         yesterday -
17   JF:   Yeah. Right.
18   MM:   So, I didn't even think - bother to schedule the Death Star. We
19         were going to work the spread -
20   JF:   Right.
21   MM:   - and then when I go to check the one hour that started -
22         started early - hour ending 12, I was like, "no!"
```

Another significant distinction between internal and external calls is the more frequent sharing of privileged information in the former. The regular exchange of sensitive and potentially incriminating information suggests two key dynamics at play within the company: a high level of mutual trust among employees and a troubling normalization of market manipulation as a standard and legitimate business strategy.

Furthermore, the 'justify' move was notably more common in internal calls. This move typically surfaced during disagreements or reflective discussions about strategic decisions. In such cases, the trustworthiness, and specifically the 'ability', of individual team members often came under scrutiny. These conversations generally centered on issues such as identifying missteps, deciding on corrective actions, and navigating challenges during the escalating California energy crisis. For example, in Extract 20, TB and JL engage in a candid conversation that reflects their attempt to rationalize and justify their actions amid regulatory pressure and ethical gray areas. JL, acknowledging the tension of operating within the limits of the system, notes the potential repercussions of their actions even when technically compliant with regulations. TB, in turn, justifies their approach by emphasizing efforts to balance economic incentives while maintaining caution (lines 32–37). This interaction underscores the ongoing tension Enron employees faced between the drive for profit maximization and the need to maintain a facade of compliance and integrity.

Extract 20. Source document: SNO-221, 04/08/2000.

```
1    TB:  Um, k -- one other thing that, ah, the regulatory's all in a
2         big concern about is we're wheeling power out of California.
3    JL:  I know, but I guess - yeah, I know. But he - ah, I - I mean you
4         - you talked with ah -
5    TB:  [surname].
6    JL:  [surname] - he sounds like he's OK with what you're doing, so.
7    TB:  Yep.
8    JL:  I mean [phone receiver picked up] you know, I've become such a
9         wooss on this stuff, too, because of this - with this Alberta
10        thing, right?
11   TB:  Yeah.
12   JL:  And ah, it's just fuckin' unfortunate - we're going to have
13        repercussions of all this stuff, and not necessarily 'cause we
14        do anything wrong. Just because these fuckin' - you know.
15   TB:  Yeah.
16   JL:  You take this much money out of a market, I think that there's
17        um, you know, they just fuckin' like try to find somethn' [sic]
18        and - and I think you guys are - he thinks you guys are doing
19        everything a - right, and being cautious, and I think that's
20        fine.
21   TB:  OK. Yeah, I just wanted to make sure you - you know, we are -
22        we're - we're -- in-in time when it's not - we're basically
23        looking at whether we think they're going to curtail our
24        exports, 'cause if the curtail 'em it fuckin' blows, 'cause
25        we're short the 250 call.
26   JL:  Right. Right.
27   TB:  Um, and ah, so we've got a big economic incentive not to abuse
28        this thing.
29   JL:  Right.
30   TB:  Um, but if it looks like they're not going to curtail 'em,
31        we're doing some size.
32   JL:  Right. Right. Um, -- I mean, if you don't do the things you're
33        allowed to do in a market-place, well, it's going to be hard to
```

```
34         make money over time, so, it's kinda hard to say, well, we
35         should be, you know, we shouldn't do this even though it's
36         allowed, because, you know, I mean, that's what we do.
37         [chuckles]
38   TB:   Right. Right.
```

The second factor we examined to understand situational variation in Enron's trust management was the overall purpose of the call. Figure 10 highlights significant differences in the distribution of moves across the five main categories, indicating that the conversation's focus and interactional goals shaped which aspects of trust were most relevant and how they were discursively managed. Perhaps unsurprisingly, 'share emotions' was by far the most prevalent move in social conversations. This highlights the important role played by these casual exchanges in fostering affective trust and alignment among Enron traders and between Enron traders and external business partners. The moves 'offer reassurance', 'show concern', and 'highlight advantages' were relatively common in calls with clients. This finding supports earlier observations about their persuasive use in projecting care and enticing clients to follow Enron's expert advice. The 'share privileged information' move was most frequent in coordinating and trading/scheduling calls, where Enron and both internal and external traders planned and jointly executed their trading strategies, including illicit ones.

Regulatory/rules calls contained a relatively high frequency of 'repair' moves, in particular 'show transparency' and 'justify'. These moves were often used alongside other defensive moves in response to direct challenges from the energy market operator ISO, such as Extracts 2 and 11. The other patterns observed in this category are less interpretable and reliable, owing to the small and varied composition of the sample, which includes fourteen conversations with regulatory bodies as well as conversations *about* regulation. Moreover, the quantitative findings for certain moves are significantly skewed by outlier interactions. For instance, SNO-192 shows a very high frequency of tokens of 'show concern for interlocutor', driven by an extended exchange where Enron's JF offers friendly advice to his colleague BW. Similarly, SNO-242 is the only conversation in this category that contains instances of 'praise'. Here, TA repeatedly praises colleague TD on his successful advocacy of Enron's interests during a recent meeting with regulators on how to best respond to the California energy crisis. TD was able to secure greater flexibility in market operations and scheduling, both of which were critical elements of Enron's trading strategy.

The final situational factor we examined was the degree of familiarity between speakers. Figure 11 highlights distinct patterns linking the use of

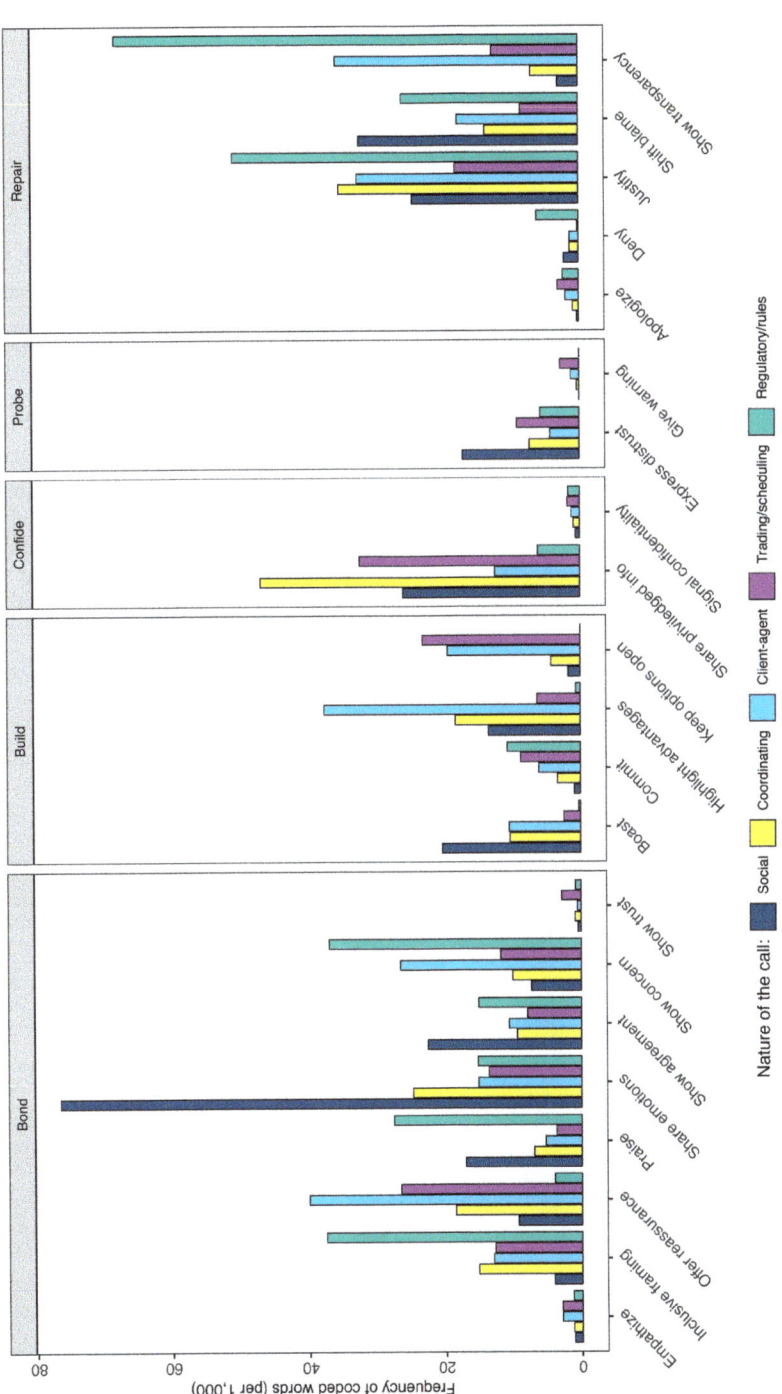

Figure 10 Distribution of trust management moves by 'nature of the call' categories. Counts refer to moves used by Enron speakers only.

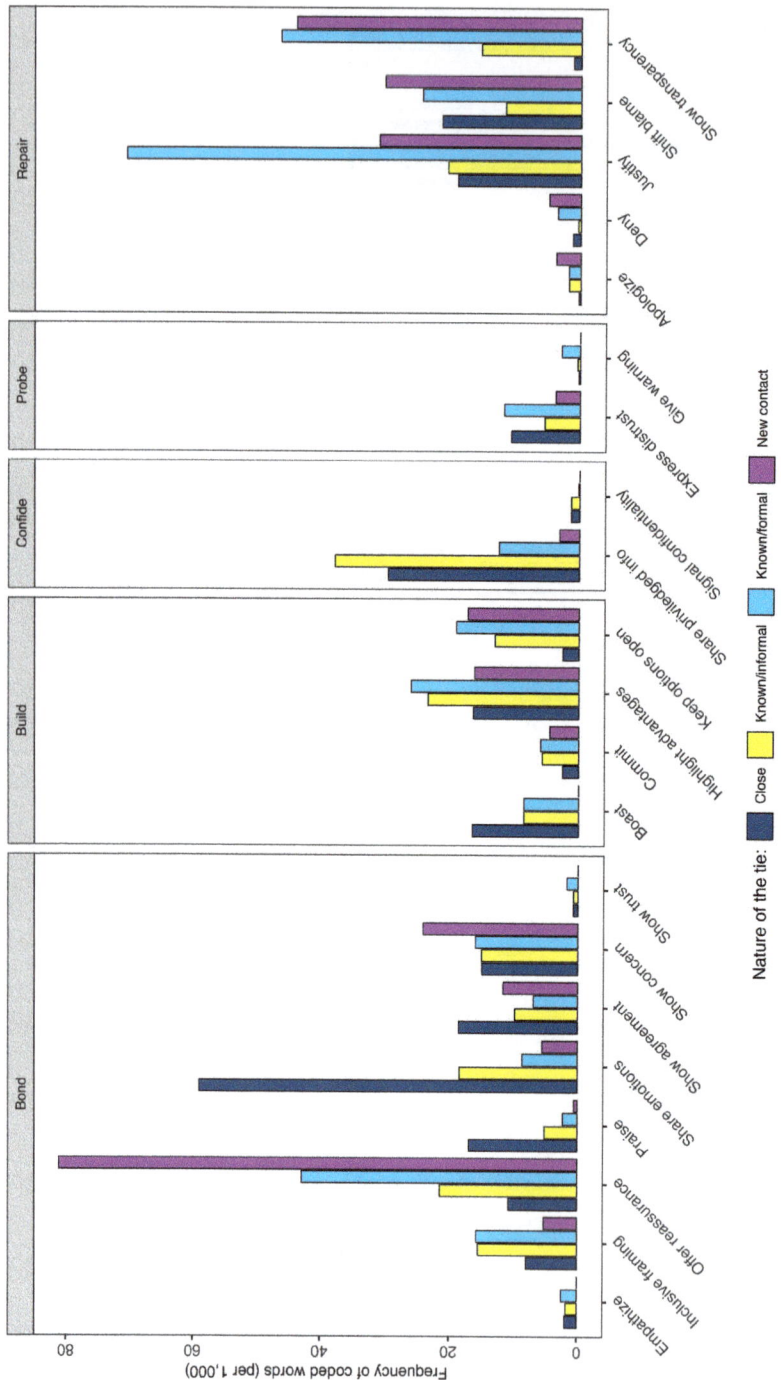

Figure 11 Distribution of trust management moves by 'nature of the tie' categories. Counts refer to moves used by Enron speakers only.

trust management strategies to the depth of the relationship between interactants. The 'share emotions' move exhibits a clear pattern; as relationships between speakers grow closer, the emotional content of their conversations increases. Conversely, the 'offer reassurance' move shows the opposite trend, indicating a greater need to proactively manage trust in less intimate relationships. Similarly, the 'justify' and 'show transparency' moves were employed more frequently in formal and less familiar relationships. Boasting and praising, on the other hand, occurred more often in close relationships, likely due to higher levels of mutual trust among close acquaintances and the function that boasting served in fostering a sense of camaraderie and shared success, as discussed above. As expected, 'sharing privileged information' was predominantly found in conversations between close acquaintances.

Overall, these findings not only provide deeper insights into how Enron managed the trust of different types of interlocutors but also lend support to the validity of our framework and its diagnostic potential. The frequency of trust management moves in the ETTC aligns well with our expectations: closer relationships exhibit language that signals a higher degree of mutual trust, especially evident in the sharing of emotions and privileged information. In contrast, less intimate relationships tend to involve more 'repair' moves and offers of reassurance, which indicate a greater need to proactively earn and maintain trust.

5.5 Move Correlations and Sequences

In addition to analyzing the frequency of each move and its distribution across different types of conversations, another valuable quantitative insight we can extract from the coded ETTC is move co-occurrence patterns. This relationship is visualized in Figure 12, where the size and color intensity of the shapes represent the strength of the correlation between the moves in our typology. The shape type indicates whether the correlation is positive or negative (circle and square, respectively). Larger and darker circles indicate a higher likelihood of the moves appearing together within the same call. For example, 'express distrust' often appears alongside 'deny' and 'justify', while 'share emotions' frequently co-occurs with 'show agreement'.

This type of analysis can help us identify recurring dialogic sequences through which participants negotiate trust as the interaction unfolds. Our analysis identifies two distinctive types of trust management sequences in the ETTC. The first, which we term 'distrust sequence', arises in situations where one speaker expresses distrust toward the interlocutor, prompting

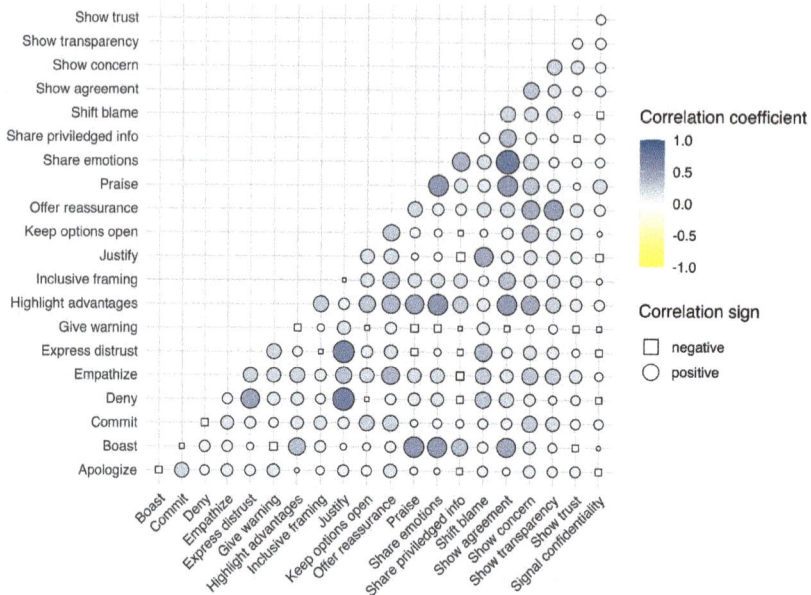

Figure 12 Correlation matrix of trust management move co-occurrences.

the latter to attempt repair. This sequence involves the move 'express distrust' alongside the 'repair' strategies 'deny', 'justify', and 'shift the blame', all of which are strongly correlated with one another. An example of this pattern is found in Extract 11, where expressions of distrust (lines 9, 12, 14, 18–20) are followed by different 'repair' moves (lines 10–11, 13, 15–17, 21).

The second type of trust management sequence revealed by the correlation plot, which we term 'bonding sequence', involves speakers building upon each other's moves to show stance alignment and affiliation. A prime example is the frequent pairing of 'share emotions' and 'show agreement'. This pattern was common in both internal and external conversations where Enron traders and their interlocutors vented frustrations about the emergency regulatory interventions planned by the State of California to address the energy crisis, as shown in Extract 3. Bonding sequences indicate and potentially foster mutual trust by promoting a sense of solidarity, emotional resonance, and ideological alignment between speakers.

Correlation analysis is not only valuable for identifying moves that tend to co-occur and form sequences, but it can also provide important theoretical insights by showing which moves do *not* correlate. For instance, Figure 12 indicates that 'boast' and 'apologize', 'express distrust' and 'inclusive framing' rarely, if ever, co-occur within our corpus. These negative correlations suggest the existence of implicit, culture- and context-specific pragmatic norms that shape how trust is discursively managed. For example, boasting after an apology might undermine the speaker's credibility by appearing insincere, as it shifts attention away from the apology and gives the impression that the speaker is more focused on self-promotion than on addressing the issue. Similarly, inclusive framing within a distrustful context may seem overly presumptuous, as it assumes a level of agreement or alignment that has not yet been established, potentially making the speaker appear out of touch with the dynamics of the conversation.

5.6 Diachronic Analysis

The final stage of the quantitative analysis focused on how Enron's trust management tactics evolved over time. Due to data sparseness and gaps, we opted to group the calls into three distinct phases, informed by a historical analysis of the California energy crisis, rather than plotting the data on a linear time scale. The first crisis period covers conversations from January to September 2000. Investigations into Enron's behavior and regulatory interventions began towards the end of this period in August and September, when most conversations included in the corpus were recorded. The second crisis period, between October 2000 and May 2001, marked a severe escalation, with Enron facing intense scrutiny and decisive regulatory interventions that stabilized energy prices. The third phase, spanning June 2001 to January 2002, captures the aftermath of the California energy crisis and the dramatic collapse and ultimate bankruptcy of the wider Enron Corporation.

Figure 13 shows a considerable decline in the relative density of discursive trust management between the first and second phase of the crisis. To complement these general statistics and gain a deeper understanding of how Enron's trust management behavior evolved during the crisis, we analyzed the relative frequency of the five macro-functions across the three phases. Figure 14 highlights a clear decrease in 'confide' moves and a sustained increase in 'repair' moves. 'Bond', initially dominant, also declines over time.

These findings, together with the general frequency trends depicted in Figure 14, suggest that in the first phase of the crisis, Enron engaged in intensive discursive trust work, heavily relying on bonding and confiding. 'Bond' moves, in particular 'share emotions' (15.21% of coded words in phase 1 versus 9.90% in phase 2 and 10.19% in phase 3), helped foster solidarity and alignment both

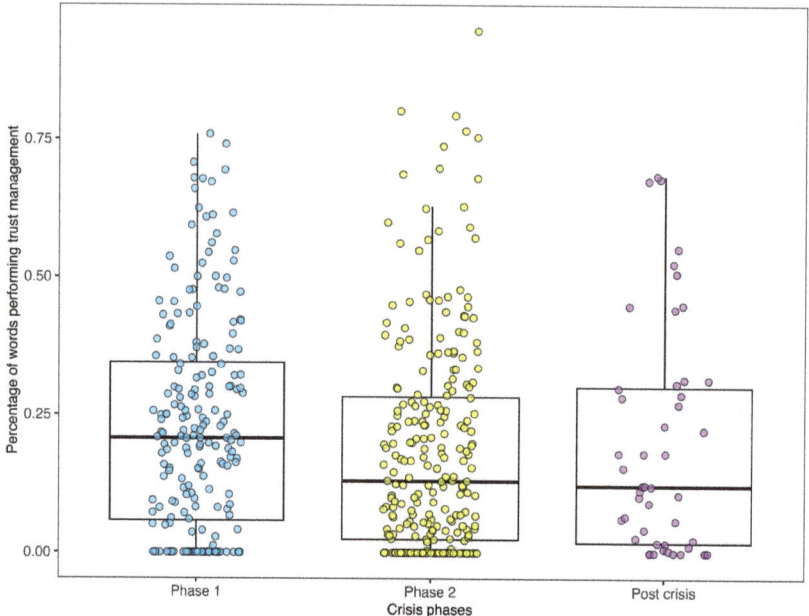

Figure 13 Frequency of trust management words across crisis phases. Counts refer to moves used by Enron speakers only.

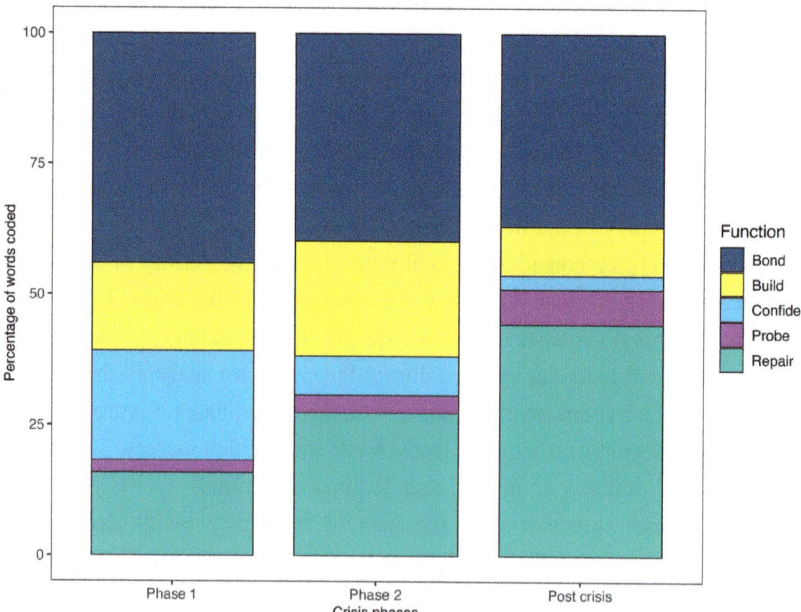

Figure 14 Distribution of trust management macro functions across crisis phases. Counts refer to moves used by Enron speakers only.

internally and between Enron and its business partners. This inward-facing approach flourished in a corporate environment driven by a shared free-market ideology. The frequent use of emotive language to express resentment toward perceived regulatory interference likely reinforced this ideology and fostered cohesion within Enron's corrupt network, uniting its members against a common adversary: the State. The exceptionally high frequency of the 'share privileged information' move during this phase – vastly exceeding that of all other phases (20.55% of coded words in phase 1 versus 6.86% in phase 2 and 2.58% in phase 3) – reflects low perceptions of risk and perhaps a sense of hubris amid the lucrative wave of market gaming, as well as the extent to which such practices had become normalized.

However, as the crisis deepened and regulatory interventions intensified, the frequency of 'confide' moves sharply declined while 'repair' moves increased. The decrease in the sharing of privileged information may indicate that established market strategies required less discussion but could also reflect heightened regulatory scrutiny, which pushed Enron toward greater secrecy. The increased frequency of 'repair' and 'build' moves suggests that trust had become more unstable and greater effort was needed to mend and sustain it. The relatively high frequency of the 'build' moves 'highlight advantages' (9.61% of coded words in phase 2 versus 7.78% in phase 1 and 4.28% in phase 3) and 'keep options open' (5.30% of coded words in phase 2 versus 3.45% in phase 1 and 1.59% in phase 3) suggest that Enron traders faced heightened resistance and needed to be particularly persuasive to convince external clients and partners to follow their lead. At the same time, the 'repair' move 'justify' was also at its highest (15.07% of coded words in phase 2 versus 5.63% in phase 1 and 13.46% in phase 3), indicating increased turmoil both internally and externally, as well as a need to rationalize potentially risky decisions in an environment of intensified scrutiny.

By the third phase, Enron's trust management behavior reflects a severe loss of credibility, driven by the combined impact of the FERC investigation, new regulatory interventions in California aimed at controlling prices, and the growing scandal engulfing the parent corporation in Houston, which ultimately led to its bankruptcy in December 2001.[2] This phase is characterized by a dominance of 'repair' moves, signaling heightened levels of distrust directed at the company and a desperate struggle to regain trust amid an escalating reputational crisis. Additionally, this phase sees an increase in 'probe' moves, primarily in the form of 'express distrust'. These instances involved remaining Enron employees voicing distrust and anger toward top executives at the center

---

[2] Enron's West Division, however, continued trading even after the parent corporation filed for bankruptcy, operating until the FERC ruling on June 25, 2003.

of the accounting scandal, as illustrated in Extract 21. In doing so, they attempted to distance themselves from the leadership in a bid to salvage a measure of trust as the West Power division struggled to navigate this challenging and uncertain period.

Extract 21. Source document: SNO-540, 09/11/2001.

```
1   SP:  Well - so, it's - ah, we're just kind of wait and see. We have
2        like absolutely no information, so we're just waiting. So, I
3        told you they were all crooks. I just didn't know how much.
4   D:   [inaudible].
5   SP:  Or how many.
6   D:   I read somewhere in the paper, what was it? The ex-executives
7        were selling all the way down from 30s and 40s or whatever?
8   SP:  Well, y - they've all - they've been selling for the last year
9        and a half, but yeah, they were continuing to sell. 'Cause they
10       knew it was about to come to a head.
11  D:   Oh, I love it. You know, this is a standard joke around town
12       now that you - you look back and - Oh! oh, there's 600 million
13       here that we - we didn't - must have forgot. You know this is
14       in the paper -
15  SP:  Well, ah, ah, yeah, it was the - all those partnerships.
16  D:   Yeah, yeah, well they just -
17  SP:  Well, no, it was off balance sheets, so they didn't have to
18       report it in their mind. It's just a big lie. I mean, it was -
19       it's just so much worse than I'd thought, you know, I'd always
20       been a cynic here and then things, you know, the last few years
21       I'd kind of turned around because I felt like a lot of good
22       things were happening, and I could see all the money that our
23       group was making a bunch of money.
24  D:   Y'all were keepin' 'em afloat.
25  SP:  Yeah, and that's what we didn't realize and they were just
26       lying to us, telling us that the other groups were doin' OK,
27       and were, you know, turnin' the corner into profitability and
28       this that and the other, you know, all the new things they were
29       gettin' into. And that was just all - I mean, I - I - I - I
30       just see, ah - see it now, all the times that we were just lied
31       right to our faces. Right here on the floor. Very informal
32       meetings they just downright lied.
```

6 Discussion

Our analysis of the Enron case study has thrown into sharp relief the pivotal role of language in managing trust within interpersonal relationships and in enabling the operation of Enron's complex corrupt network. In this section, we reflect on the insights gained from the analysis in relation to the two research questions posed at the outset of this Element.

6.1 How Do Speakers Manage Trust in Interaction?

Previous research in forensic linguistics and discourse analysis highlights the pivotal role of language as a tool for trust building. However, existing studies have primarily focused on a narrow set of context-specific features and do not offer a comprehensive, general-purpose framework for studying discursive trust management. To address this gap and develop a new approach that broadens our understanding of the linguistic and pragmatic mechanisms of trust, we posed a simple yet fundamental question: what are the discursive strategies that speakers commonly employ to manage trust in interaction?

Drawing on an interdisciplinary methodology that combines move analysis with theoretical insights on trust from the behavioral sciences, we have identified twenty-one pragmatic moves routinely used by speakers to manage trust in interaction. Furthermore, we propose that discursive trust management boils down to five core processes or 'macro functions' – 'bond', 'build', 'confide', 'probe', and 'repair' – to which the moves can be mapped. Our framework represents the first comprehensive effort to systematize the pragmatics of trust. It captures the diverse ways in which speakers discursively manage trust and provides a versatile tool for further research across different communicative contexts.

Several moves included in our typology were identified in earlier work and proved equally crucial in the Enron case study. Lorenzo-Dus and Izura (2017) highlighted the role of praising as a key trust-building strategy. Lorenzo-Dus et al. (2023) found that online groomers often share personal information and intimate details about romantic relationships to entice children, a strategy that fits with our 'confide' macro-function. Romantic scammers' manipulative self-disclosure narratives heavily rely on emotive language (Carter 2024) and can thus be seen as an instance of the 'share emotions' move. The detailed accounts of drug-related experiences used by drug traffickers on the Dark Web to communicate competence (Lorenzo-Dus & Di Cristofaro 2018) match our 'boast' move category. Our study consolidates these insights into a unified, coherent analytical framework, while also expanding the range of discursive trust management strategies considered. Moreover, by drawing on well-established theoretical principles from trust research, our framework offers a more precise understanding of the specific facets of trustworthiness that different moves are designed to target.

Our analysis reinforces the centrality of emotions and bonding in discursive trust management (Lorenzo-Dus et al. 2023; Wang & Yao 2022). The prevalence of 'bond' moves in our corpus demonstrates that trust is fundamentally both cognitive and affective (McAllister 1995). That is, trust emerges not only from a rational assessment of how trustworthy someone is, but also from the emotional connection and sense of security and comfort we *feel* with them. Notably, our analysis shows that even in professional contexts like energy trading, this affective dimension remains essential. By adopting a broad perspective that considers both cognitive and affective moves, our framework captures the intricate interplay between 'cognitive-based' and 'affect-based' trust and illustrates how both are actively managed through discourse.

Beyond providing a comprehensive inventory of the moves speakers use to manage trust in interaction, our analysis offers broader theoretical insights into the relationship between discourse and trust. First, discourse is not merely a tool to persuade others to trust us; it is the primary "site" where trust is *interactively* negotiated. As observed in our data, speakers use language both to affirm their own trustworthiness and to evaluate that of their interlocutors. They dynamically adapt to each other's contributions, leveraging the shared discursive context they co-construct to inform their next actions. This context serves as the foundation for interpreting, evaluating, and continually revising their mutual perceptions of trustworthiness as the interaction unfolds. This co-construction of trust manifests most clearly in specific interactional sequences, such as those discussed in Section 5.5. Trust, therefore, is not merely a pre-existing condition reflected in discourse, but something that is actively created and maintained through communication. In other words, discourse is not just reflective but *constitutive* of trust. While non-discursive realities and material actions undoubtedly influence trust decisions, it is through discourse that individuals collaboratively interpret these experiences, assess their relevance, and negotiate their "diagnostic potential" for trustworthiness. This is shown most clearly in Extracts 12 and 13, where the speakers seek to reconcile divergent understandings of a potentially trust-damaging event – an anomaly in Enron's web-based trading platform.

Another key theoretical insight emerging from our analysis is the close relationship between interpersonal and situational trust, the latter defined as implicit expectations about the predictability of social behavior and mutual understanding. Our findings reveal that when material events deviate from these expectations, they can prompt a re-evaluation of an interlocutor's trustworthiness and subsequent discursive renegotiation of trust. This dynamic is seen repeatedly in our data, including in Extract 11, where a power generator is unexpectedly cut off, in Extract 12, where a sudden price jump occurs, and in Extract 18, where unexpected contract details emerge. In all these cases, perceived deviations from normalcy prompt discursive trust repair efforts led by the speaker acting as the trustee in that specific context. This dynamic highlights the dual nature of trust: it hinges not only on impressions of a person's trustworthiness but also on the predictability of the surrounding context – both of which are mediated through discourse.

Situational trust extends beyond the predictability of material behavior and real-world situations to include the predictability of communication itself. This is captured by the linguistic concept of 'genre', which establishes recognizable patterns and conventions that signal the nature and purpose of text or talk, creating a framework of expectations for both senders and receivers. It is no coincidence, then, that one of the most effective strategies in scams involves mimicking the genre conventions of legitimate forms of communication, such as official government letters, corporate emails, bank statements, and so on. By replicating these familiar conventions, scammers exploit situational trust to manipulate their targets.

Our analysis also reveals that, just as trust is inherently context-dependent (Mayer et al. 1995: 726–727), so too is its discursive management. As demonstrated in our analysis, Enron traders' trust management strategies varied significantly across different interactional contexts and types of relationships. For instance, in interactions with clients, traders predominantly employed 'bond' moves such as 'offer reassurance' and 'show concern', emphasizing care and interest. In contrast, trading and regulatory calls featured a higher frequency of 'repair' moves, particularly 'show transparency' and 'justify'. This variation underscores how the context – including the purpose of the interaction, the identity of the interlocutor, and the depth of the relationship – determines which aspects of trustworthiness are most salient, thereby influencing linguistic behavior. In client interactions, benevolence appears to take precedence, prompting Enron traders to focus on projecting genuine care and goodwill. Meanwhile, in conversations with institutional and oversight entities like the ISO, integrity was the priority, with traders emphasizing transparency and good faith. Ultimately, this highlights the performative nature of discursive trust management, particularly in professional settings such as this one. Speakers adapt their roles and personas to fit different contexts (Goffman 1959), and this is also reflected in their trust management discourse. By emphasizing the facets of trustworthiness most relevant to the context, speakers actively shape relationships in ways that facilitate mutual understanding and the achievement of their goals.

Lastly, our analysis confirms our initial expectation that trust is not solely managed discursively for manipulative purposes, a focus that has dominated forensic linguistics thus far. In many cases, Enron traders fostered positive, mutually beneficial relationships with a range of clients and business partners. These relationships were built on a shared value system and a free-market ideology within which the actions of both Enron and its partners were considered legitimate and largely unproblematic. In such contexts, bonding emerged as the predominant form of discursive trust management. While we cannot access the inner thoughts of Enron speakers, it is reasonable to infer that much of this bonding work was genuine and grounded in ideological alignment rather than manipulation or deception. This seemingly mundane trust-building, however, was far from trivial; instead, it provided fertile ground in which corruption and wrongdoing eventually took root. Recognizing that trust management is not always inherently manipulative is therefore crucial, particularly when analyzing complex forms of criminal activity that involve networks of multiple parties with diverse roles and relationships.

6.2 How Did Enron Traders use Language to Manage the Trust of Relevant Parties in Executing their Illicit Market Manipulation?

Our analysis reveals four key mechanisms through which Enron traders discursively managed trust while manipulating California's energy markets: (i) fostering ideological alignment and in-group solidarity, (ii) projecting competence and benevolence, (iii) managing information disclosure, and (iv) defending legitimacy when challenged. Together, these mechanisms enabled Enron to execute its market gaming tactics while maintaining the trust of key stakeholders, at least until the crisis and subsequent regulatory intervention exposed and ultimately unraveled the company's wrongdoing.

A central feature of Enron's trust management strategy was the cultivation of ideological alignment and in-group solidarity. With close business partners, Enron traders used 'bond' moves like 'share emotions' and 'show agreement' to create a sense of unity against perceived common adversaries, namely California State regulators. The emotional intensity of these exchanges, evident in the frequent use of swearing and other emotive language, helped cement affective bonds between participants while reinforcing their shared ideological stance.

Ideological alignment was also constructed through recurring narratives that framed California's regulatory interventions as irrational and unwarranted interference with market forces. These narratives helped legitimize the exploitation of California's newly deregulated energy markets or Enron-sanctioned responses to the business risks they were perceived to have created. Organizational research emphasizes that, in many cases, acts that constitute or contribute to wrongdoing are significantly influenced by how a given situation is framed, with the capacity for neutralizing or rationalizing language to reduce the moral intensity of problematic decisions or even render decision-makers unaware of any wrongful implications (De Klerk 2017; Kump & Scholz 2022). By drawing on a known case of corporate corruption that was, in the main, dialogically coordinated and enabled, our analysis provides insights into how this phenomenon occurs linguistically and the implicit connection it has to interpersonal trust. In particular, we show how Enron's traders discursively framed the reasonableness of actions that deviated from energy scheduling norms (e.g., misstating generation intentions) or had the capacity to exacerbate the crisis situation (e.g., exporting energy outside California).

The cultivation of in-group solidarity was particularly evident in internal conversations among the energy traders, where sharing emotions and mutual praise helped promote a corporate culture that normalized and celebrated aggressive market behavior while fostering strong interpersonal bonds. The frequent use of 'praise' and 'boast' moves in internal calls points to a reward system where market manipulation success garnered peer recognition and status. The discursive practice of flaunting and celebrating the successful execution of gaming strategies likely helped override individual moral concerns by recasting questionable actions as the innovative enactment of their professional role. Thus, the successful use of trading strategies was often the subject of praise and admiration rather than scrutiny. This dynamic may have helped create a self-reinforcing cycle: successful manipulation led to praise from peers, which encouraged further manipulation, leading to more praise and the increased normalization of corruption over time (Ashforth & Anand 2003; Palmer 2012).

Taken together, these trust management strategies can be seen as geared towards fostering or leveraging 'identification-based trust', a deep and robust form of trust based on mutual empathy, shared values, and emotional connection that enables parties to understand, align with, and act on each other's behalf (Lewicki & Bunker 1996). This form of trust was not, of course, a characteristic of all the relationships Enron traders maintained with external actors. It is more evident in interactions among traders themselves and with close external partners.

The second pillar of Enron's trust management strategy shaped external perceptions among clients and business partners through language that conveyed both competence ('ability') and genuine care ('benevolence'). This approach was particularly evident in interactions with clients who maintained less intimate, more formal relationships with Enron and, thus, were among those with little or no apparent understanding of the company's market manipulation schemes. Traders used moves like 'highlight advantages', 'keep options open', 'inclusive framing', and 'offer reassurance' to present themselves as not only knowledgeable and technically competent but also genuinely committed to maximizing benefits for their clients. These moves appear designed to foster 'knowledge-based' trust, a cognitive form of trust that arises from having sufficient information to understand and accurately anticipate the likely actions of others (Lewicki & Bunker 1996). Their effectiveness was likely amplified by the overarching professional credibility of the Enron corporation, underscoring the dynamic interplay between 'interpersonal' and 'institutional' trust. The company's established reputation for success, coupled with reassurances of benevolence and partnership offered by Enron traders, likely persuaded clients unfamiliar with both Enron and the new market-based environment to follow their advice, particularly in the early days of the newly deregulated California energy markets. These findings demonstrate that the role of discursive trust management in corruption extends beyond collusive trust (i.e., trust in participants' discretion and good faith toward illicit endeavors) to include the manipulation of others' actions through the trust typically associated with professional relationships (c.f. Muzio et al. 2011).

This dual ability-benevolence approach was also strategically important in navigating the escalating California energy crisis. Enron traders worked to contain client concerns about the negative effects of the crisis and the State's regulatory interventions, while simultaneously diverting attention from the fact that those adverse effects were partly a result of the very strategic market moves they were implementing. Lastly, the combination of ability and benevolence was also instrumental in securing compliance from external partners. Since Enron did not own any energy-producing facilities, control of client generation, transmission, and scheduling arrangements was a vital component in its traders' ability to enact their market manipulation strategies. This was especially evident in the strategic use of 'inclusive framing', which reframed controversial decisions as collaborative ventures. This tactic fostered a sense of partnership in decision-making, earning client trust even as Enron exploited that trust for its own gain, and its actions undermined market stability and, at times, its clients' own interests as a result. These tactics reveal a manipulative aspect of Enron's trust management, where language was used to subtly persuade external actors, such as utilities and power generation facilities, to execute market moves aligned with Enron's strategic goals.

The third major component of Enron's overall trust management approach involved the strategic management of sensitive information. By selectively sharing details of their market gaming strategies, traders created mutual vulnerability with collaborating parties while demonstrating trust in their discretion, which arguably strengthened their bond. This information sharing was calibrated based on relationship depth and conversation context. The analysis shows 'confide' moves were predominantly used with close contacts and in coordination-focused and trading calls. Traders would share sensitive information about strategies with trusted contacts while maintaining stricter information control with less familiar parties. This selective transparency created circles of trust that facilitated market manipulation while managing the risk of exposure. The evolution of information-sharing practices throughout the crisis reveals sophisticated adaptation to changing circumstances. The sharp decline in the frequency of the 'share privileged information' move as regulatory scrutiny increased demonstrates how traders adjusted their disclosure practices to balance trust maintenance with risk management.

Finally, the analysis clearly demonstrates that trust in Enron was neither inherent nor stable and grew increasingly strained as the crisis unfolded. To navigate this situation, Enron traders engaged in substantial discursive efforts to maintain and restore trust with various external stakeholders. In their interactions with clients, they employed a suite of defensive strategies that reframed their actions as legitimate. These included invoking market logic (e.g., adhering to "price signals"), exploiting regulatory ambiguities (operating in "gray areas"), and attributing blame to external factors (such as California's flawed market design, "forcing" certain behaviors). This layered approach to defense helped sustain trust by offering multiple justifications for their conduct while reinforcing ideological alignment with their interlocutors. When directly confronted by agents of the market operators, ISO and PX, traders deployed coordinated sequences of defensive trust repair moves. These included denying misconduct, presenting alternative explanations, and redirecting blame to external entities. Together, these tactics helped them maintain an appearance of legitimacy and mitigate reputational damage as they pursued their wrongful activities.

These four mechanisms did not operate in isolation but formed an integrated system of trust management that enabled Enron's market manipulation. Ideological alignment created the foundation for trust by establishing shared worldviews and values. The projection of competence and benevolence built on this foundation by positioning Enron as a capable and caring market actor. Strategic information management strengthened relationships while controlling risk, and the legitimation and trust-repair strategies helped maintain trust when challenges arose. The effectiveness of this trust management system is evident in how long Enron was able to sustain its market manipulation despite growing evidence of misconduct. The traders' ability to adapt their linguistic strategies based on audience, context, and crisis phase helped maintain necessary trust relationships even as external pressures mounted.

7 Conclusion

This Element has proposed a new framework for analyzing discursive trust management and has illustrated its use through the analysis of one of the most notorious and impactful instances of corporate misconduct in history: Enron West Power's manipulation of California's energy markets. Our analysis not only provides novel insights into the Enron case but also advances our understanding of the linguistic and pragmatic foundations of trust and the relationship between discourse, trust, and corporate corruption. The Enron Trader Tapes Corpus, which we have compiled for this study and made publicly accessible for research purposes, represents a major new resource for forensic linguistics and discourse analysis. Access to such clandestine conversations is rare, and existing datasets are often limited in scope, making the ETTC an invaluable asset for both this specific case study and forensic linguistics more broadly.

The primary aim of our framework is to provide a comprehensive account of the repertoire of discursive strategies available to speakers to manage trust in interaction. While some features we discuss have been documented in prior research, ours is the first effort to systematize the pragmatics of trust into a versatile analytical tool that may be used to study discursive trust management in a wide range of communicative contexts. In forensic contexts, the framework can unlock new perspectives that deepen our understanding of various forms of wrongdoing. In the specific case of corporate corruption analyzed here, our findings reveal some of the discursive mechanisms that enable and legitimize wrongful behavior within an organization and show how trust management operates as a highly flexible tool to secure cooperation, whether others are complicit in the wrongdoing or unaware of its ethical or legal implications.

Novel insights could be gained by applying this framework to other wrongful, harmful, or illicit activities, both in the real world and cyberspace. These include emerging forms of online radicalization, such as those fostered through extremist discussion forums, ideological harm networks like incel communities and the broader "manosphere", and different kinds of fraud, such as impersonation scams, phishing schemes, and social engineering tactics where perpetrators pose as authorities or trusted entities to exploit their victims. In each of these contexts, trust and discourse are pivotal in enabling harmful actions, manipulating victims, and fostering cooperation between individuals in pursuit of common ideological or illicit goals.

Crucially, beyond advancing theoretical understanding of these phenomena, the analysis of discursive trust work could inform practical interventions to address these emerging challenges. For example, our analysis demonstrates that by examining language, we can infer the level of trust between individuals, which in turn can help us identify the roles and relationships within a specific criminal network. Similarly, studying the trust dynamics within extremist or ideological harm networks online could deepen our understanding of how and why individuals are drawn to these groups and guide the development of well-informed social policies and educational interventions.

Analysis of discursive trust management in these and other forensic contexts will contribute to consolidating, refining, and expanding our framework. While comprehensive, our model should be viewed as a preliminary proposal rather than a definitive account of all the pragmatic moves involved in discursive trust management. It is likely that additional trust management moves exist that were not included here because they did not occur in the specific communicative context we have analyzed. Furthermore, some of the macro-functions and moves identified in our corpus may manifest in context-specific forms in other scenarios. For example, romantic scams often involve the elicitation and exchange of messages and images of a sexual nature (Carter 2024). These discursive practices can be interpreted as a context-specific instantiation of the 'bond' macro-function, designed to foster affective trust by simulating physical intimacy.

In addition to testing the model in different contexts, another important direction for future research is to look beyond moves to examine other, more fine-grained linguistic features that may play a significant role in discursive trust management. One of the key insights from our analysis is the importance of emotive language as a discursive engine of trust. Future work may explore this aspect further, employing, for example, the appraisal framework (Martin & White 2005) or Bednarek's corpus-assisted approach to 'emotion talk' (Bednarek 2008) to investigate how emotive language is used to promote and consolidate affective trust. The role of humor and laughter, closely tied to emotion, is also likely important in this respect and may serve as an indicator of high levels of mutual trust. These elements were prominent in our corpus, particularly in conversations between close acquaintances. Similarly, terms of address, as highlighted at the outset of this Element, and discourse markers such as "well", frequently observed in interactional sequences marked by disagreement and distrust, emerge as promising focal points for further enriching our understanding of discursive trust management at a more granular level.

Taking this finer-grained perspective further, the study of discursive trust management would benefit greatly from the adoption of a conversation analytical approach. In this Element, we have employed a discourse analysis approach informed by move analysis. This method was chosen for two reasons: first, to map the discursive dynamics of trust over a large corpus and provide a comprehensive picture of the Enron case study; second, because the transcripts we analyzed, while of high quality, lack the level of detail and accuracy required for a fully-fledged conversation analysis. Conversation analysis could complement this approach by offering deeper insights into the mechanics, sequences, and micro-level features of discursive trust management. A glimpse of this potential is evident in our brief analysis of the role of affiliation (e.g., Couper-Kuhlen 2012; Stivers 2008) in 'bonding' sequences. Conversation analysis could extend this by shedding light on features not considered here, such as pauses, epistemics, and non-verbal cues like gestures, facial expressions, and body language. These elements are likely to play an integral role in trust management and merit further exploration.

A significant limitation of our approach is that it relies on labor-intensive manual coding. Manual analysis is necessary because the linguistic categories of interest extend beyond individual lexical units and lack unequivocal mapping to specific lexical forms. These characteristics make it challenging to automate the analysis while ensuring high accuracy and coverage. However, recent studies show that large language models (LLMs) can achieve human-level accuracy in discourse annotation tasks, such as coding the pragmatic elements of apologies (Yu et al. 2024) and, more relevantly, moves in research article abstracts (Yu et al. 2024). Future research should therefore investigate the potential of LLMs to automate and scale up the application of our annotation system. The potential of this approach extends far beyond our framework because the challenges that limit the automation of our analysis are shared by many discourse annotation tasks. If successful, LLM-assisted annotation could significantly reduce the time and cost of discourse annotation and open up new opportunities for large-scale corpus research across various forensic linguistic and discourse analytical contexts, such as the rhetorical moves employed by child sexual offenders on the dark web (Chiang et al. 2021) or the power dynamics in extremist forums (Newsome-Chandler & Grant 2024).

In conclusion, this Element has highlighted the central role of discourse in building, maintaining, and manipulating trust. Our framework provides a systematic tool for examining how language shapes trust relationships, enabling different forms of unlawful and harmful activities. By uncovering some of the linguistic mechanisms through which trust is negotiated, this work advances theoretical understanding and offers practical insights for addressing trust-related challenges in forensic contexts. We hope that this framework will serve as a foundation for future studies and practical applications, contributing to both academic knowledge and real-world efforts to understand and address the role of language in trust dynamics.

References

Anderson, A., & Petersen, A. (2013). Nanotechnologies and trust. In C. N. Candlin & J. Crichton (eds.), *Discourses of Trust* (pp. 237–251). Palgrave.

Antaki, C., & Finlay, M. L. W. (2013). Trust in what others mean: Breakdowns in interaction between adults with intellectual disabilities and support staff. In C. N. Candlin & J. Crichton (eds.), *Discourses of Trust* (pp. 21–35). Palgrave.

Ariely, D. (2012). *The (Honest) Truth about Dishonesty: How We Lie to Everyone, Especially Ourselves*. HarperCollins.

Ashforth, B., & Anand, V. (2003). The normalization of corruption in organizations. *Research in Organizational Behavior*, 25, 1–52.

Ashforth, B., Gioia, D., Robinson, S., & Trevino, L. (2008). Re-viewing organizational corruption. *Academy of Management Review*, 33(3), 670–684.

Baker, P., Vessey, R., & McEnery, T. (2021). *The Language of Violent Jihad*. Cambridge University Press.

Balleisen, E. (2018). *Fraud: An American History from Barnum to* Madoff. Princeton University Press.

Bednarek, M. (2008). *Emotion Talk across Corpora*. New York and Basingstoke: Palgrave Macmillan.

Benítez-Castro, M.-Á., & Hidalgo-Tenorio, E. (2022). "I Am Proud to Be a Traitor": The emotion/opinion interplay in jihadist magazines. *Pragmatics and Society*, 13(3), 501–531.

Benke, G. (2018). *Risk and Ruin: Enron and the Culture of American Capitalism*. University of Pennsylvania Press.

Bertrand, O., & Lumineau, F. (2016). Partners in crime: The effects of diversity on the longevity of cartels. *Academy of Management Journal*, 59(3), 983–1008.

Bhagwat, A. (2003). Institutions and long term planning: Lessons from the California electricity crisis. *Administrative Law Review*, 55(1), 95–125.

Bhatia, V. K. (1993). *Analysing Genre: Language Use in Professional Settings*. Longman.

Biber, D., Ulla, C., & Upton, T. A. (2007). *Discourse on the Move: Using Corpus Analysis to Describe Discourse Structure*. John Benjamins.

Black, W., Calavita, K., & Pontell, H. (1995). The savings and loan debacle of the 1980s: White-Collar crime or risky business? *Law & Policy*, 17(1), 23–55.

Blumstein, C., Friedman, L., & Green, R. (2002). The history of electricity restructuring in California. *Journal of Industry, Competition and Trade*, 2(1), 9–38.

Bondi, M., & Nocella, J. J. (2023). Building trust in the transport sector during the pandemic: A cross-cultural analysis. *Language and Dialogue*, 13(3), 309–335.

Brown, P., & Levinson, S. C. (1987). *Politeness: Some Universals in Language Usage* Cambridge University Press.

Bruijne, M. (2009). Enron. In E. Heuvelhof, M. Jong, M. Kars, & H. Stout (eds.), *Strategic Behaviour in Network Industries: A Multidisciplinary Approach*. Edward Elgar.

Carter, E. (2024). *The Language of Romance Crimes: Interactions of Love, Money, and Threat*. Cambridge University Press.

Chiang, E., & Grant, T. (2017). Online grooming: moves and strategies. *Language and Law*, 4(1), 103–141.

Chiang, E., Nguyen, D., Towler, A., Haas, M., & Grieve, J. (2020). Linguistic analysis of suspected child sexual offenders' interactions in a dark web image exchange chatroom. *International Journal of Speech, Language and the Law*, 27(2), 129–161.

Chiang, E., Nguyen, D., Towler, A., Haas, M., & Grieve, J. (2021). Linguistic analysis of suspected child sexual offenders' interactions in a dark web image exchange chatroom. *The International Journal of Speech, Language and the Law*, 27(2), 1-33.

Childs, C., & Walsh, D. (2017). Self-disclosure and self-deprecating self-reference: Conversational practices of personalization in police interviews with children reporting alleged sexual offenses. *Journal of Pragmatics*, 121, 188–201.

Cook, K. S. (2001). *Trust in Society*. Russell Sage Foundation.

Costa, A. C., Fulmer, C. A., & Anderson, N. R. (2018). Trust in work teams: An integrative review, multilevel model, and future directions. *Journal of Organizational Behavior*, 39(2), 169–184.

Couper-Kuhlen, E. (2012). Exploring affiliation in the reception of conversational complaint stories. In M.-L. Sorjonen & A. Peräkylä (eds.), *Emotion in Interaction* (pp. 113–146). Oxford University Press.

Crichton, J. (2013). Will there be flowers shoved at me?' A study in organisational trust, moral order and professional integrity. In C. N. Candlin & J. Crichton (eds.), *Discourses of Trust* (pp. 119–132). Palgrave.

De Klerk, J. J. (2017). "The devil made me do it!" An inquiry into the unconscious "devils within" of rationalized corruption. *Journal of Management Inquiry*, 26(3), 254–269.

Dietz, G., & Den Hartog, D. N. (2006). Measuring trust inside organisations. *Personnel Review*, 35(5), 557–588.

Du Bois, J. W., Schuetze-Coburn, S., Cumming, S., & Paolino, D.anae (1993). Outline of discourse transcription. In Jane A. Edwards & Martin D. Lampert, eds., *Talking Data: Transcription and Coding in Discourse Research*. Hillsdale, NJ: Lawrence Erlbaum. 45–89.

Etaywe, A., & Zappavigna, M. (2022). Identity, ideology and threatening communication: An investigation of patterns of attitude in terrorist discourse. *Journal of Language Aggression and Conflict*, 10(2), 315–350.

Etaywe, A., & Zappavigna, M. (2024). The role of social affiliation in incitement: A social semiotic approach to far-right terrorists' incitement to violence. *Language in Society*, 53(4), 623–648.

Federal Energy Regulatory Commission (FERC). (2003a). Commission revokes Enron's Market-based Rate Authority, Blanket Gas Certificates Terminated [Press Release].

Federal Energy Regulatory Commission (FERC). (2003b). Order Revoking Market-Based Rate Authorities and Terminating Blanket Marketing Certificates.

Federal Energy Regulatory Commission (FERC). (2007). Initial Decision.

Fogarty, K., Augoustinos, M., & Kettler, L. (2013). Re-thinking rapport through the lens of progressivity in investigative interviews into child sexual abuse. *Discourse Studies*, 15(4), 395–420.

Forney, J. (2000). Email to Miller, Rosman, Wolfe and Foster re "Here's some service for you!". 4 Feb. 2000, EL03-180, SNO-98, FERC.

Fulmer, C. A., & Gelfand, M. J. (2012). At what level (and in whom) we trust: Trust across multiple organizational levels. *Journal of Management*, 38(4), 1167–1230.

Fuoli, M. (2018a). A stepwise method for annotating appraisal. *Functions of Language*, 25(2), 229–258.

Fuoli, M. (2018b). Building a trustworthy corporate identity: A corpus-based analysis of stance in annual and corporate social responsibility reports. *Applied Linguistics*, 39(6), 846–885.

Fuoli, M., Van De Weijer, J., & Paradis, C. (2017). Denial outperforms apology in repairing organizational trust despite strong evidence of guilt. *Public Relations Review*, 43(4), 645–660.

Garfinkel, H. (1963). A conception of, and experiments with "trust" as a condition of concerted stable actions. In O. J. Harvey (ed.), *Motivation and Social Interaction* (pp. 187–238). Ronald Press.

Goffman, E. (1959). *The Presentation of Self in Everyday Life*. Bantam Doubleday Dell Publishing Group.

Goldfarb, B., & Kirsch, D. (2019). *Bubbles and Crashes: The Boom and Bust of Technological Innovation*. Stanford University Press.

Graeff, P. (2004). Why should one trust in corruption? The linkage between corruption, norms and social capital. In J. G. T. Lambsdorff, M. Schramm, &

M. T. Boyce (eds.), *The New Institutional Economics of Corruption* (pp. 67–90). Routledge.

Greve, H., Palmer, D., & Pozner, J. (2010). Organizations gone wild: The causes, processes, and consequences of organizational misconduct. *The Academy of Management Annals*, 4(1), 53–107.

Groom, N., & Grieve, J. (2019). The evolution of a legal genre: rhetorical moves in British patent specifications, 1711 to 1860. In T. Fanego & P. Rodríguez-Puente (eds.), *Corpus-based Research on Variation in English Legal Discourse* (pp. 201–234). John Benjamins.

Hall, C., Mäkitalo, Å., Slembrouck, S., & Doherty, P. (2013). Pursuing trust in child protection meetings: Familiarisation and informality. In C. N. Candlin & J. Crichton (eds.), *Discourses of Trust* (pp. 100–118). Palgrave.

Hewett, D. G., M., W. B., & Gallois, C. (2013). Trust, distrust, and communication accommodation among hospital doctors. In C. N. Candlin & J. Crichton (eds.), *Discourses of Trust* (pp. 36–51). Palgrave.

Isaeva, N., Gruenewald, K., & Saunders, M. N. (2020). Trust theory and customer services research: theoretical review and synthesis. *The Service Industries Journal*, 40(15–16), 1031–1063.

Johnson, A., & Wright, D. (2014). Identifying idiolect in forensic authorship attribution: An n-gram textbite approach. *Language and Law*, 1(1), 37–69.

Khodyakov, D. (2007). Trust as a process: A three-dimensional approach. *Sociology*, 41(1), 115–132.

Kump, B., & Scholz, M. (2022). Organizational routines as a source of ethical blindness. *Organization Theory*, 3(1), 1–24.

Kuśmierczyk, E. (2014). Trust in action: Building trust through embodied negotiation of mutual understanding in job interviews. In K. Pelsmaekers, G. Jacobs, & C. Rollo (eds.), *Trust and Discourse: Organizational Perspectives* (pp. 11–44). John Benjamins.

Ladd, B. K., & Goodwin, J. (2022). Extreme arguments: Anwar al-Awlaki's radicalizing discourse. *Journal of Pragmatics*, 200, 39–48.

Lewicki, R. (2006). Trust, trust development, and trust repair. In M. Deutsch & P. T. Coleman (eds.), *The Handbook of Conflict Resolution: Theory and Practice* (pp. 92–119). Jossey-Bass Publishers.

Lewicki, R. J., & Bunker, J. Z. (1996). Developing and maintaining trust in work relationships. In R. M. Kramer & T. R. Tyler (eds.), *Trust in Organizations: Frontiers of Theory and Research* (pp. 114–139). Sage.

Linell, P., & Keselman, O. (2011). Trustworthiness at stake: Trust and distrust in investigative interviews with Russian adolescent asylum-seekers in Sweden. In I. Marková & A. Gillespie (eds.), *Trust and Conflict: Representation, Culture and Dialogue* (pp. 156–181). Routledge.

Lorenzo-Dus, N. (2022). *Digital Grooming: Discourses of Manipulation and Cyber-Crime*. Oxford University Press.

Lorenzo-Dus, N., & Di Cristofaro, M. (2018). "I know this whole market is based on the trust you put in me and I don't take that lightly": Trust, community and discourse in crypto-drug markets. *Discourse & Communication*, 12(6), 608–626.

Lorenzo-Dus, N., Evans, C., & Mullineux-Morgan, R. (2023). *Online Child Sexual Grooming Discourse*. Cambridge University Press.

Lorenzo-Dus, N., & Izura, C. (2017). "Cause ur special": Understanding trust and complimenting behaviour in online grooming discourse. *Journal of Pragmatics*, 112, 68–82.

Lorenzo-Dus, N., Izura, C., & Pérez-Tattam, R. (2016). Understanding grooming discourse in computer-mediated environments. *Discourse, Context & Media*, 12, 40–50.

Lorenzo-Dus, N., & Kinzel, A. (2019). "So is your mom as cute as you?": Examining patterns of language use in online sexual grooming of children. *Journal of Corpora and Discourse Studies*, 2(1), 1–30.

Lorenzo-Dus, N., Kinzel, A., & Di Cristofaro, M. (2020). The communicative modus operandi of online child sexual groomers: Recurring patterns in their language use. *Journal of Pragmatics*, 155, 15–27.

Lorenzo-Dus, N., & Macdonald, S. (2018). Othering the West in the online Jihadist propaganda magazines *Inspire* and *Dabiq*. *Journal of Language Aggression and Conflict*, 6(1), 79–106.

Lorenzo-Dus, N., & Nouri, L. (2021). The discourse of the US alt-right online – a case study of the *Traditionalist Worker Party* blog. *Critical Discourse Studies*, 18(4), 410–428.

Macdonald, S., & Lorenzo-Dus, N. (2021). Visual: Constructing the "good muslim" in online *Jihadist* magazines. *Studies in Conflict & Terrorism*, 44(5), 363–386.

Maclean, M., Harvey, C., & Clegg, S. R. (2016). Conceptualizing historical organization studies. *The Academy of Management Review*, 41(4), 609–632.

Marková, I., & Gillespie, A. (2008). *Trust and Distrust: Sociocultural Perspectives*. Information Age.

Martin, J. R., White, P. R.R. (2005). *The Language of Evaluation: Appraisal in English*. Palgrave Macmillan, London and New York.

Mayer, R. C., & Davis, J. H. (1999). The effect of the performance appraisal system on trust for management: A field quasi-experiment. *Journal of Applied Psychology*, 84(1), 123–136.

Mayer, R. C., Davis, J. H., & Schoorman, F. D. (1995). An integrative model of organizational trust. *The Academy of Management Review*, 20(3), 709–734.

McAllister, D. J. (1995). Affect- and cognition-based trust as foundations for interpersonal cooperation in organizations. *The Academy of Management Journal*, 38(1), 24–59.

Mollin, S. (2007). The Hansard hazard: gauging the accuracy of British parliamentary transcripts. *Corpora*, 2(2), 187–210.

Muzio, D., Kirkpatrick, I., & Kipping, M. (2011). Professions, organizations and the state: Applying the sociology of the professions to the case of management consultancy. *Current Sociology*, 59(6), 805–824.

Newsome-Chandler, H., & Grant, T. (2024). Developing a resource model of power and authority in anonymous online criminal interactions. *Language and Law / Linguagem e Direito*, 10(1), 110–130.

Nix, A., & Decker, S. (2023). Historical methods and approaches to researching organizational wrongdoing. In M. Clemente, C. Gabbioneta, & R. Greenwood (eds.), *Research in the Sociology of Organizations: Organisational Wrongdoing* (pp. 141–158). Emerald.

Nix, A., Decker, S., & Wolf, C. (2022). Enron and the California energy crisis: The role of networks in enabling organizational corruption. *Business History Review*, 95(4), 765–802.

O'Grady, C., & Candlin, C. N. (2013). Engendering trust in a multiparty consultation involving an adolescent patient. In C. N. Candlin & J. Crichton (eds.), *Discourses of Trust* (pp. 52–69). Palgrave.

Pablos-Ortega, C. de. (2021). Mitigation and aggravation in police investigative interviews: "Would it be fair to say that you actively sought out material?" In L. Filipović (ed.), *Police Interviews: Communication Challenges and Solutions* (pp. 51–72). John Benjamins.

Palmer, D. (2008). Extending the process model of collective corruption. *Research in Organizational Behavior*, 28, 107–135.

Palmer, D. (2012). *Normal Organizational Wrongdoing: A Critical Analysis of Theories of Misconduct in and by Organizations*. Oxford University Press.

Pechman, C. (2005). Supplemental testimony of Carl Pechman, PhD. *On Behalf of Public Utility District*, (1). EL03-180, SNO-160, 2007.

Pinto, J., Leana, C., & Pil, F. (2008). Corrupt organizations or organizations of corrupt individuals? Two types of organization-level corruption. *Academy of Management Review*, 33(3), 685–709.

Pounds, G. (2019). Rapport-building in suspects' police interviews: The role of empathy and face. *Pragmatics and Society*, 10(1), 95–121.

Prentice, S., Rayson, P., & Taylor, P. J. (2012). The language of Islamic extremism: Towards an automated identification of beliefs, motivations and justifications. *International Journal of Corpus Linguistics*, 17(2), 259–286.

QSR International. (2022). NVivo (Version 13, 2020 R1).

Rhodes, C. (2016). Democratic business ethics: Volkswagen's emissions scandal and the disruption of corporate sovereignty. *Organization Studies*, 37(10), 1501–1518.

Rousseau, D. M., Sitkin, S. B., Burt, R. S., & Camerer, C. (1998). Not so different after all: A cross-discipline view of trust. *Academy of Management Review*, 23(3), 393–404.

SNOPUD. (2007). Reply brief of public utility district no. https://elibrary.ferc.gov/idmws/search/fercgensearch.asp.

Spadaro, G., Gangl, K., Prooijen, J. W., Lange, P. A., & Mosso, C. O. (2020). Enhancing feelings of security: How institutional trust promotes interpersonal trust. *PLoS One*, 15(9), 1–22.

Spencer-Oatey, H. (2008). *Culturally Speaking: Culture, Communication and Politeness Theory*. Continuum.

Spooren, W., & Degand, L. (2010). Coding coherence relations: Reliability and validity, 6(2), 241–266.

Stivers, T. (2008). Stance, alignment, and affiliation during storytelling: When nodding is a token of affiliation. *Research on Language and Social Interaction*, 41(1), 31–57.

Swales, J. M. (1990). *Genre Analysis: English in Academic and Research Settings*. Cambridge University Press.

Upton, T. A., & Cohen, M. A. (2009). An approach to corpus-based discourse analysis: The move analysis as example. *Discourse Studies*, 11(5), 585–605.

Wang, X., & Yao, H. (2022). In government microblogs we trust: Doing trust work in Chinese government microblogs during COVID-19. *Discourse & Communication*, 16(6), 716–734.

Weare, C. (2003). *The California Electricity Crisis: Causes and Policy Options*. Public Policy Instit. of CA.

Wilson, L., & Walsh, D. (2019). Striving for impartiality: Conflicts of role, trust and emotion in interpreter-assisted police interviews. *Pragmatics and Society*, 10(1), 122–151.

Wright, D. (2013). Stylistic variation within genre conventions in the Enron email corpus: developing a textsensitive methodology for authorship research. *International Journal of Speech Language and the Law*, 20(1), 45–75.

Yu, D., Bondi, M., & Hyland, K. (2024). Can GPT-4 learn to analyse moves in research article abstracts? Applied Linguistics, amae071. https://academic.oup.com/applij/advance-article-abstract/doi/10.1093/applin/amae071/7863767.

Acknowledgments

We are grateful to Alejandro Napolitano Jawerbaum for his work in pre-processing the corpus, preparing it for release, and assisting with the extraction of speaker turn word counts. We also thank Ellen Wilding for her help with processing the annotated Nvivo files, and Major Pau for contributing to the literature review on corporate corruption. Finally, we are indebted to Marcus Perlman, Jack Grieve, Tim Grant, and two anonymous reviewers for their insightful and constructive feedback on earlier versions of this work.

Cambridge Elements

Forensic Linguistics

Tim Grant
Aston University

Tim Grant is Professor of Forensic Linguistics, Director of the Aston Institute for Forensic Linguistics, and past president of the International Association of Forensic Linguists. His recent publications have focussed on online sexual abuse conversations including *Language and Online Identities: The Undercover Policing of Internet Sexual Crime* (with Nicci MacLeod, Cambridge, 2020).

Tim is one of the world's most experienced forensic linguistic practitioners and his case work has involved the analysis of abusive and threatening communications in many different contexts including investigations into sexual assault, stalking, murder, and terrorism. He also makes regular media contributions including presenting police appeals such as for the BBC Crimewatch programme.

Tammy Gales
Hofstra University

Tammy Gales is Professor of Linguistics and the Director of Research at the Institute for Forensic Linguistics, Threat Assessment, and Strategic Analysis at Hofstra University, New York. She has served on the Executive Committee for the International Association of Forensic Linguists (IAFL), is on the editorial board for the peer-reviewed journals Applied Corpus Linguistics and Language and Law / Linguagem e Direito, and is a member of the advisory board for the BYU Law and Corpus Linguistics group. Her research interests cross the boundaries of forensic linguistics and language and the law, with a primary focus on threatening communications. She has trained law enforcement agents from agencies across Canada and the U.S. and has applied her work to both criminal and civil cases.

About the Series

Elements in Forensic Linguistics provides high-quality accessible writing, bringing cutting-edge forensic linguistics to students and researchers as well as to practitioners in law enforcement and law. Elements in the series range from descriptive linguistics work, documenting a full range of legal and forensic texts and contexts; empirical findings and methodological developments to enhance research, investigative advice, and evidence for courts; and explorations into the theoretical and ethical foundations of research and practice in forensic linguistics

Cambridge Elements

Forensic Linguistics

Elements in the Series

Forensic Linguistics in the Philippines: Origins, Developments, and Directions
Marilu Rañosa-Madrunio, Isabel Pefianco Martin

The Language of Fake News
Jack Grieve, Helena Woodfield

A Theory of Linguistic Individuality for Authorship Analysis
Andrea Nini

Forensic Linguistics in Australia: Origins, Progress and Prospects
Diana Eades, Helen Fraser, Georgina Heydon

Online Child Sexual Grooming Discourse
Nuria Lorenzo-Dus, Craig Evans and Ruth Mullineux-Morgan

Spoken Threats from Production to Perception
James Tompkinson

Authorship Analysis in Chinese Social Media Texts
Shaomin Zhang

The Language of Romance Crimes: Interactions of Love, Money, and Threat
Elisabeth Carter

Legal-Lay Discourse and Procedural Justice in Family and County Courts
Tatiana Grieshofer

Forensic Linguistics in China: Origins, Progress, and Prospects
Yuan Chuanyou, Xu Youping and Lu Nan

Decoding Terrorism: An Interdisciplinary Approach to a Lone-Actor Case
Julia Kupper, Marie Bojsen-Møller, Tanya Karoli Christensen, Dakota Wing, Marcus Papadopulos and Sharon Smith

Trust, Discourse, and Corporate Corruption: The Case of Enron
Matteo Fuoli, Adam Nix, Alicia Wickert, and Annina Van Riper

A full series listing is available at: www.cambridge.org/EIFL

For EU product safety concerns, contact us at Calle de José Abascal, 56–1°,
28003 Madrid, Spain or eugpsr@cambridge.org.

www.ingramcontent.com/pod-product-compliance
Ingram Content Group UK Ltd.
Pitfield, Milton Keynes, MK11 3LW, UK
UKHW021614130126
466887UK00014B/218